EVERY CHILD MATTERS

EVERY CHILD MATTERS

Kailash Satyarthi
Nobel Peace Laureate

PRABHAT
PRAKASHAN

Published by
PRABHAT PRAKASHAN PVT. LTD.
4/19 Asaf Ali Road,
New Delhi-110 002 (INDIA)
e-mail: prabhatbooks@gmail.com

ISBN 978-93-5266-638-6
EVERY CHILD MATTERS
by Shri Kailash Satyarthi

Edition
2026

Price
₹ 600.00 (Rupees Five Hundred only)

Printed at
R-Tech Offset Printers, Delhi

Contents

Interviews

Preface

I treasure many memorable days of my life. One of them was at Chennai in September, 2017 during the Bharat Yatra I had led against child sexual abuse and trafficking. While addressing a jam-packed auditorium, I watched a young boy walk up and greet me. With a firm nod of his head, the boy introduced himself and announced, "I am Satyarthi." Smiling indulgently, I said, "I really like your name, my friend. Do you have any other name?" With passion and determination in his eyes, Satyarthi told me that his parents had named him Abdul. He added, "But now onwards, I am Satyarthi. I listened to you and realised that you speak in our voice for children like me everywhere. From now on, I am Satyarthi." Abdul Satyarthi was just one of the tens of thousands of young boys and girls who met me and inspired me during the Yatra that travelled 12,000 kilometres across India. It is these children who give hope that we dare to dream of a better future.

I dream of a world full of safe children and safe childhoods. As I often say, I dream of a world where every child enjoys the freedom to be a child. I have no doubt that humanity can be redeemed and can prosper only when we nurture safe childhoods. For thousands of years, we, as adults, have contaminated and even destroyed childhoods by injecting fear, greed and prejudice into the minds of children. I visualise a future where children retain their unique traits of truthfulness, pure anger, fearlessness and innate compassion even as they become physically old. This prompts us to say that divinity is reflected in a pure form only in children. When we speak of a happy adult, we say she is laughing like a child. When we praise an adult, we remark on her child-like simplicity and innocence. I don't want children to lose these traits as they grow up. In fact, I consider myself to be a 64-year-old child.

People familiar with my work at the grassroots level know how long and arduous the journey has been, but it has been immensely satisfying. When I first rescued children being forced to work as slaves, I had not imagined that the struggle for fundamental rights and safety of children would become a global movement. Even within India, we have won many victories along the way. At every step, when we were confronted by vested interests, we took the initiative and knocked on the doors of the judiciary, pushing and prodding courts across India to demand justice. And we won many landmark cases along the way. I have been campaigning against child marriage for decades. So it was a heartening moment recently when the Supreme Court delivered a verdict that categorises sex with a minor wife as statutory rape. Till a few years ago, nobody bothered about hundreds of thousands of children from poor families who went missing. In most cases, the police did not even register the report. A majority of these children fell prey to trafficking gangs. But thanks to the judiciary once again, India is getting a handle on this menace. In 2017, after years of persuasion, the Government of India finally ratified Conventions 138 and 182 of the International Labour Organisation that prohibits the worst form of child labour. When crime data for 2016 were released late last year by the NCRB (National Crime Records Bureau), the initial reaction in media was about the steep rise in crimes against children. It is indeed a serious problem. But it is also a fact that after POCSO (Protection of Children from Sexual Offences Act) was enacted in 2012, victims and family members are breaking their silence and speaking out.

As important as judicial intervention has been the increasing social awareness and mass mobilisation to secure fundamental rights of children. Across India and the world, civil society organisations and movements have played a significant role in promoting and protecting the rights of children. In many cases, they have been joined enthusiastically by ordinary citizens, who want a better and safer future for their children. What is also heartening is that many governments have shed their historical indifference of the past and become more responsive, coming out with policies and schemes tailor-made to benefit poor and deprived children. Even as I write this, an anti-trafficking Bill is being readied to be tabled in the Parliament.

And yet, despite many victories, we still confront significant challenges when it comes to safe children and safe childhoods. Millions of children in war-torn countries have either been killed or have become homeless refugees, vulnerable to trafficking gangs. There seems no solution in sight. Even today, about 600 million children live in poverty, while 152 million children are being forced to work as child labour. More than 60 million children have dropped out of school. In a large number of countries, including India, the state of public health and education is so pathetic that poor children are being denied a dignified future. Even today, apathy looms large. It would take just about $ 40 billion to ensure universal education. We still struggle to find those funds even as we spend 50 times as much on the Armed Forces.

But there is light at the end of this tunnel. We have collectively demonstrated that change is possible. In just about one-and-half decades, our persistent efforts have reduced the number of child workers from 268 million to 152 million at the global level. Our constant campaigns to encourage children to access quality education has resulted in the number of school dropouts falling even faster from 130 million to 60 million. I am optimistic that child labour will be eliminated in my life-time. No doubt, humanity faces many dangers caused by ecological damage, civil wars and conflicts and geo-political challenges, but together, we can overcome them and leave a safer world for our children. The key lies in globalising compassion.

This collection of articles and some interviews reflect the achievements and challenges. I am sure you will find them interesting as well as illuminating. I would urge each one of you to become an ambassador and a warrior for child rights because after all, every child matters.

— Kailash Satyarthi

1
Children Need Global Help

Every year, as the global community gears up to commemorate June 12 as the World Day against Child Labour, my memories go back 19 years to those electrifying few months in 1998 when our movement for child rights won not just a tangible victory, but also a moral crusade. That was when like-minded people across the world forged a truly global partnership to organise the Global March against Child Labour.* When it culminated at Geneva, even we were pleasantly surprised by the reaction of the almost 2,000 delegates, including labour ministers from 150 countries, who had gathered there for the annual meeting of the International Labour Organisation.

Not only did 600 children and activists who had marched across the world get a standing ovation, but the ILO (International Labour Organisation) actually agreed to pass an international legislation on worst forms of child labour. The popularly known Convention 182 was adopted unanimously the following year. At one stroke, the global community made a sincere and honest attempt to stop an abomination that haunted and troubled the conscience of the world: the pernicious and unacceptable violation of child rights. By then, we had spent 18 struggling but satisfying years fighting against child labour through our organisation

* Almost two decades ago, the Global March against Child Labour led to momentous changes. But while much has been achieved, children still need a coordinated global effort to secure their future.

'Bachpan Bachao Andolan', which was launched in 1980. The quick decision by the ILO to declare exploitative child labour as illegal made our struggle worth it. Subsequently, the decision in 2002 to mark June 12 every year as the World Day against Child Labour ensures that the global community remains engaged and focussed on abolishing child labour.

Indeed the global community needs to retain unwavering focus. By 1990, the United Nations had announced that all children would get education by the year 2000, but nothing of that sort was happening at the ground level. By 1996, it was estimated that about 250 million children were being exploited through child labour, millions of them as virtual slaves or bonded labour. Freedom, education and basic rights were a distant dream for these 250 million children. However, much to our satisfaction, the situation started improving at the ground level. There was a significant drop in the prevalence of child labour for a decade or so. But, much to our dismay, that is no longer true. The last four years have actually seen stagnation, if not an increase in the prevalence of child labour. On the eve of the World Day against Child Labour in 2016, the United Nations officially reported that 168 million children across the world were still being ruthlessly exploited despite stringent laws against child labour.

To this dangerous ground-level situation has been seen an alarming increase in recent years of child refugees and trafficking. Children constitute one-third of the total population of the world, but account for more than 50 per cent of refugees. In the last 10 years, close to 10 million children have been killed in conflicts and more than six million have become physically disabled. It is estimated that 28 million children have become refugees without any hope for a future. Syria and Afghanistan alone accounted for more than 50 per cent of child casualties and refugees in 2015. While accurate and reliable numbers are not available, there is a consensus that the refugee crisis has led to a big jump in child-trafficking.

Clearly, the global community needs to engage and focus all over again with a sense of urgency on the menace of child labour and trafficking. The menace must be tackled in a multi-dimensional manner. We need to partner more effectively with spiritual leaders to raise awareness. No religion sanctions the exploitation of children; rather, all of them consider protection of children as a sacred duty. Apart from religion, we need to address this issue at a cultural level too. In virtually every society, ranging from the so-called primitive to the most advanced, children are treasured and celebrated. We need to channelise these cultural legacies into a sustained movement, both at the local community as well as the global level.

Religion and culture give us the moral foundation to build a better world for our children. Economics will provide the means and resources to do the same. It has been established that acute lack of livelihood opportunities often leads to child labour. Targeted welfare schemes, like the NREGA and the Mid-Day Meals Scheme have not only led to a dramatic rise in enrolment of children in schools, but also a drop in child labour. But this economic struggle is going to be long and arduous. Even today, it has been estimated that more than 600 million children suffer from extreme poverty. Education is the way out of this morass. No civilised society can justify child labour when it is the biggest impediment to education, which remains the most effective, enabling, equalising and empowering force. Besides, what moral argument can anyone put forth when more than 210 million adults remain jobless even as 168 million children are forced into child labour? Our moral challenge is to ensure that the next generation doesn't suffer the same fate.

I remain optimistic. Our march in 1998 saw tens of thousands of ordinary citizens in cities like Dhaka, Oslo, Sao Paolo, Paris, Bangkok, Capc Town and Kabul among others actively participating and demanding abolition of child labour. One of the most evocative slogans then was: From Exploitation to Education. The time has come to launch yet another major global effort.

❑

2
Choosing the Right Heroes

Dear young friends,

It has been 68 years since India won independence from the British rule. Many countries have got their independence before and after India, but our freedom struggle and hopes have been different from others.*

The courageous, legendary and visionary leaders of our freedom struggle might have had two distinct ideologies and approaches to attaining freedom. But their definition of freedom was never limited to overthrowing the British. It was more comprehensive and stretched wider.

That definition included education and freedom for all, abolition of untouchability, *gram swaraj* (village independence) to socialism, decentralisation of power and effective democracy. Most of these principles and aspirations have been weaved wonderfully in our Constitution.

However, through waves of time, the notion of freedom has become shrunken and superficial.

Today, while celebrating Independence Day, we should not forget the original idea of freedom. Today, let us remind ourselves of our countrymen who have still not tasted freedom.

Some of those people who celebrated August 15, 1947 are still not free. Moreover, their second or third generations

---

* This column was written on the eve of the 68th Independence Day of the country. It exhorts the youth to launch a mass movement against brutal exploitation of young girls.

are born enslaved to their landlords and masters. I have myself freed grandparents, parents and children from bonded labour.

I am speaking of children who are forced to live away from their families to toil in mines, quarries and brick kilns, who suffer burns while making firecrackers in factories, who work around toxic chemicals, who get cuts while stitching our shoes and footballs.

I am speaking of those children who work in carpet, leather, iron and plastic factories to make products for us, who starve to serve us in hundreds of *dhabas* and restaurants in our country, who miss school to embroider our wedding trousseau. They have no childhood freedom.

I am reminding you of those lakhs of our daughters and sisters who are being sold and brought for less than the price of animals.

Isn't this an absurd joke for one of the oldest civilisations and the largest democracy that ever existed?

I want to mention here the story of a girl Meena, born in a poor family in Assam. She was kidnapped and trafficked to Delhi, where she was as a domestic labour and faced regular abuse at the hands of her employers. She did not receive a single penny for her work and was even raped.

By the time my organisation 'Bachpan Bachao Andolan' could rescue Meena, then 17, she was traumatised and had suicidal tendencies. She was also pregnant. At the time of rescue, when her father broke down looking at her and tried to hug her, she withdrew from him because she thought she was impure.

I refuse to accept that a girl can be called impure because of the wrongs of a man.

According to the latest government figures, there was a 50 per cent increase in the number of cases of crime against children between 2012 and 2013. Six children go missing every hour in India. As per Census 2011, 43.5 lakh children are working as child labourers. But according to non-governmental sources, this number is grossly underestimated and is almost five crores.

Government admits that half of all children, about to finish eight years of schooling, have still not learned basic skills in arithmetic, like subtraction and division.

The irony is that this apathy prevails in a country full of youngsters. India has the highest number of young people in the world: around 40 per cent of its population. Despite this golden chance, India currently ranks 135 among 196 countries in the Human Development Index. It ranks among countries with the largest number of child labourers.

Friends, till each child born in India gets a free, safe, healthy and respectful childhood, we cannot call our country completely free. The freedom struggle led by figures, such as Mahatma Gandhi, Bhagat Singh, Subash Chandra Bose, Chandrashekhar Azad and Ashfaqulla Khan, and many more, is still not over.

They were the freedom fighters of the past, but you can be the freedom fighters of today.

No segment of age has more energy, enthusiasm and idealism than you, the youth.

Wherever nations have risen against oppression and injustice, it has been because of the youth. The recent Arab spring, the protests in Hong Kong, Wall Street are a few examples of the power that they wield. In the remotest of areas, in the poorest of countries, youth with the support of education are raising their voices against century-old superstitions and regressive customs.

It is this potential that I sense in the Indian youth. The situation today is very different from that of 1947. The Indian youths are more educated, well-travelled, well-read and globally aware, than they have ever been. The IT revolution and the fast climb of Indians in corporate ladders everywhere have changed the reputation of our country from a land of snake charmers to a land of unmatched talent.

This youth population is not just our prized demographic dividend but also the biggest moral force.

Let us begin by choosing the right heroes for this moral force. Heroes on the silver screen or on the sports ground are no longer enough. Recognise and cultivate the hero inside you. Each one of you has a leader, a change-maker, a nation-builder inside you. Just find the right means and opportunity to translate this into action.

Speak out when you see any injustice against a child around you. Use the power of social media to bring this to the notice of the authorities. Refuse to have a glass of water at a home where a child works or a restaurant that employs child labour. Whenever you spot a child with an adult who looks suspicious at a public place, report it to the authorities.

Many of you must be voters. Use the power of your vote to choose a leader who prioritises education, health and freedom of children. Celebrate Republic Day, Independence Day, Diwali, Eid and Christmas by sharing festivities with a deprived child. Along with bringing in cheer with your family, spend ten minutes to make an unknown child smile.

I feel tremendously empowered and inspired meeting young people right from the villages to the institutes of excellence. One thing is common between the two: Young people are hungry to make India better.

Each one of you can do it. If not you, then who, if not now, then when?

Warmly,
Kailash

❑

3

Finally, Reason to Rejoice for the Children of India

After a long wait of almost two decades, the Government of India has ratified the International Labour Organisation (ILO) Convention 182 on the Worst Forms of Child Labour and Convention 138 on Minimum Age of Employment. Though belated, the decision to ratify two key ILO conventions on child labour makes clear India's intent of zero tolerance for the exploitation of children.*

I remember how we conceived this idea to demand an international law on the abolishment of modern forms of slavery, sale and trafficking of children, forced or compulsory labour and the usage of children in conflict, for pornography and for procuring and doing other illicit activities, such as drug trafficking. We conceptualised a march which would travel through 103 countries and across 80,000 kms to culminate on June 6, 1998 in Geneva, where the ILO (International Labour Organisation) was meeting for its annual conference.

Nearly 1.5 million people across the world walked together to demand a strong international law to protect vulnerable children. We even received support from 72 parliamentarians who raised the issue in their own

---

* This column was written soon after the Government of India ratified Conventions 182 and 138 of the International Labour Organisation that prohibits the worst forms of child labour. It also highlights the challenges that lie ahead.

constituencies and at the international stage. Most importantly, I remember the children who joined us from Nepal, Pakistan, Vietnam, Brazil and many such developing nations. Their presence in the seminar hall where the delegates were meeting made all the difference. The innocent, yet powerful, voices of the children could not be ignored and reflected in the draft of the ILO Convention 182 on the worst forms of child labour.

A year later, in June 1999, the ILO unanimously adopted the convention. It was the first time that a convention or treaty had been adopted with the full support of all members. Over the years, with the support of our international partner organisations, I have spearheaded its ratification by member nations. With 180 countries having already become signatories to it, the C182 has also become the fastest ratified convention in the history of the ILO. Their affiliation to the Convention clearly demonstrates the rising status of children's issues in political and global agenda.

But even as hope soars, the realities around us are a somewhat harsh reminder of the atrocities our children are subjected to. This year, particularly, I have been in anguish due to the repeated and frequent reports of sexual violence against children in India. Brutal incidents of child sexual abuse have become all too common across the country. This reveals a disturbing phenomenon which mirrors the growing frustration of our society. Today, one in every three rape victims in India is a child. According to data compiled by the NCRB (National Crime Records Bureau) for 2015, 8,800 cases of child rape were registered under POCSO. The same set of data also reveals that sexual abuse and kidnapping account for 81 per cent of the crimes against children. Going by media reports, the numbers must have increased in the past two years.

Another point of worry is the socio-economic state of Indian children. Recently, a report by the Oxford University has concluded that 31 per cent of the world's children living in abject poverty are living in India. In effect, that is more than 100 million children whose life-long potential and ability to rise out of poverty is diminished forever, because of the dearth of facilities, opportunities and a safe and nurturing childhood.

India, by the sheer strength of its numbers, resources and investments is an emerging world leader. Therefore, in order to lead the way for other nations and achieve the Sustainable Development Goals by the year 2030, protection and promotion of children's rights should be put at the top of our development agenda. This moment, which has come at the most opportune time to commemorate the World Day against Child Labour, is a testament to India's renewed commitment to end forced labour, modern slavery and human trafficking. I am hopeful that we will sustain this momentum and work towards complete elimination of all forms of violence against children.

To revive and reawaken the positive energy unleashed in 1998, we are organising a march this year christened '100 Million for 100 Million'. Our goal is to inspire, exhort and persuade 100 million young global citizens to support efforts that will ensure 100 million children are not denied their fundamental right to education. I am confident this march too will make a significant difference. I urge all to make this the last generation that witnesses child labour.

❑

4

How My Life Changed

It makes compelling and fascinating story when we talk about that one dramatic moment which fundamentally changed our lives.* The well-known thinker and writer Nassim Nicholas Taleb has coined the term 'Black Swan' which has become popular across the world. No doubt, many of us do come across such life-altering moments that persuade us to re-examine our priorities, our goals and even the path that we pursue. But more often than not, our lives are changed not by just one spectacular moment, but a more mundane procession of moments. Often, our goals, dreams and ambitions change gradually till we reach a stage where there is complete clarity about who we want to be and what we want to do.

The first such moment for me came on the first day of my school. As I was about to enter school, I saw a young boy polishing shoes along with his father. Hardly aware of the bitter realities of life like poverty, caste and discrimination, I asked my teacher that why this boy wasn't in the classroom like me. He casually answered, "It has always been like this." I found it difficult to accept this answer. I failed to get any satisfactory answer from elders in my family. Only day I walked up to the son and father and asked the father why he was not sending his son to school. For upper-caste

---

* A deeply emotional and personal account of some incidents and events that propelled the author to dedicate his life as a crusader of child rights. It reveals how he revolted against dogma and prejudice.

children, like in small towns in India, who came from families with secure, albeit modest incomes, going to school was as natural as playing with friends after school. The father looked at his son, looked again at me and mournfully pointed out that he was destined to polish shoes and school was not for children like his son. For the first time in my young life, I realised that reality was different from the comfort of a safe home and fun with your friends. I was six-years old then.

Though I couldn't yet grasp the deep-rooted resonance of the terms, I was confronted with the notions of inequality, injustice and illiberalism. In many ways, the encounter with the young boy polishing shoes outside our school sowed the seeds that would eventually determine the course of my future life.

That was the time I also found tremendous comfort in the power of compassion. Me and some of my friends organised football tournaments to raise money for poor children; we launched a drive to open libraries for them and did all we could to provide them with free books. The sparkling smiles of just a handful of poor children gave me a glimpse into a world of compassion. Of course, I wasn't old enough or angry enough to declare an open revolt against the injustice I saw around me. Yet, poor children working in shops, bus stands, railway stations and in markets continued to trouble me.

Troubled as I was, my life continued its middle-class path towards education and a secure job. Like hundreds of thousands of young Indians, I completed a degree in engineering after school and got a safe and secure job as a teacher in the engineering college. Like millions of young Indians, I got married. Perhaps my life would have continued down the path of middle-class anonymity and security, but in hindsight, I realise that the sight of that young boy polishing shoes outside my school continued to haunt me. By the time I was doing my job, my heart and soul were revolted by the sweeping injustice that I saw everywhere around me.

I was repelled by the condescending and cruel attitude of upper-caste people like me who simply accepted that poor children are born to work and not go to school and pursue their own dreams. I was revolted by the collective apathy that I saw all around me. By then, I had read a lot and come across harrowing tales of whole families working as bonded labour in brick kilns, stone quarries and numerous factories. It was all these moments of despair and an increasing urge to do something concrete about it that finally culminated in me abandoning my cushioned middle-class existence and becoming what is now fashionably called a child rights activist.

Life almost always offers us choices. Our futures are determined by the choices we make. I am glad I could muster the courage to do what I did. Children are the essence of our civilisation. If we don't treat them well, then it is rotten. In my own small way, I have spent close to 40 years trying to stem the rot.

❑

5

India Fights Back Against Child Sex Abuse

There is always a tantalising hint of dazzling light at the end of a tunnel.* Every time injustice, brutality and inhumanity raise their head, voices of protest and defiance emerge from the wilderness of despair. The voices resound when they get a platform that encourages people to walk away from fear towards freedom. Something similar is happening with the horrific and growing instances of child sex abuse and trafficking across India. Anguished as I am at the depravity of the monsters that prey on children, the courage displayed by victims, their parents, fellow citizens and the occasional display of compassion by law enforcement officials and the justice delivery system makes me hopeful that India can fight and end this menace.

Make no mistake, this is a menace that stalks and haunts all of us in India. Children are being abused in slums as well as gated communities; they are being abused in poorly run public schools to very expensive private schools; they are being abused by neighbours and relatives, tailors, software professionals, teachers and tutors. It seems, poor or rich, no one is safe. Parents worry when their children don't come back home on time. They have reason to be

---

* This column was written well before the author announced the launch of the historic Bharat Yatra against the menace of child sexual abuse and highlights how and why this needs urgent attention.

worried. Everyday, 50 cases of child sex abuse are being reported. That means two innocent and vulnerable children are violated every hour. The actual numbers are far higher as a majority of cases still don't get reported because victims and parents choose silence over pursuit of justice. It has been estimated that about 100,000 children go missing every year, with about 50 per cent never being recovered from the clutches of traffickers.

Can we make India safe for children? It looks like a long and hard battle lies ahead of us, but there are some early signs of encouragement — of victims gathering the courage to speak out; parents going to the police and of good Samaritans helping out. You might have read about the 16-year-old girl from Hyderabad who was married off to a 65-year-old citizen of Oman. The police are now pursuing the matter because the mother of the girl protested. Then, a brave young lady in Chandigarh reacted with courage and intelligence when she was stalked and almost kidnapped by two young men who happened to belong to influential families. Thanks to public and media outrage, the culprits were arrested and face trial. Early this year in Delhi, neighbours heard loud voices of protest of two young girls from near a deserted house. Thanks to the courage of the girls and the timely intervention by neighbours, a person called Sunil Rastogi was arrested before he could rape the girls. Subsequent investigations revealed that he was a serial rapist who had already abused dozens of young girls. Then again, two teenaged girls in Uttar Pradesh confronted some hoodlums stalking and eve-teasing them and ensured their arrest. These are heartening signs amidst despair.

Let me also point out how some individual police officers are helping rescue children from becoming victims of traffickers. The Vijay Vihar police station in the Rohini area of Delhi registered 82 cases of missing children in six years. Nothing much happened. Then in June 2016, a team of three police officials decided to take proactive and concerted action. Thanks to their admirable tenacity, 77 of the 82 children were rescued in just six months and reunited with their families. Then again, there is Rekha Mishra who is an inspector posted at the CST Station in Mumbai. In just one year, she has successfully prevented 434 children from becoming victims of trafficking gangs. Law enforcement officials like this give us immense hope that we can together fight this menace. Yet another positive development has been reported from Kolkata. In a landmark order, a court there has awarded ₹ 3 lakhs as interim compensation to a young girl who was trafficked and sold to a brothel in Delhi four years ago. Rescued by good Samaritans and the police and back with her family, the victim is now pursuing studies.

There is light indeed at the end of the tunnel. But I must remind everyone that we need a mass movement and mass awareness campaign across India to stop horrific incidents of trafficking and child sex abuse. Let's collectively help India fight back.

❑

6
Let's Move Beyond Rhetoric and Rituals

For India to have a future, our children deserve a present that is safer, healthier and more empowering.

We Indians seem to have a peculiar gift of transforming solemn and celebratory occasions into sham rituals devoid of any real substance. This Children's Day,* let us focus on fundamental rights of our children and their future instead of giving long speeches.

As I travelled 12,000 kilometres across India on the Bharat Yatra against child sexual abuse and trafficking, I noticed two things: Indian children are bubbling and bursting with dreams and aspirations. But we are failing them politically, economically, socially and legally. India doesn't have a future if we imperil the present of our children.

I have been fighting for children for almost 40 years now. There have been times when apathy, indifference and hostility have depressed me. But I have never lost hope in the power, faith and resolve of ordinary people to create a better future. We often fail as a society, but we also offer tantalising glimpses of our ability to nurture greatness against all odds.

---

* This column was written on Children's Day in 2017. It argues how real change must come from within and how society must move beyond paying mere lip service to child rights and their safety.

Look at the inspiring story of Dr B.R. Ambedkar, who faced a bleak future as a Dalit child facing caste discrimination. And yet, he became one of the founders of modern India. It was the access to education that transformed his life and the future of India. We need to make such individual cases of inspiration into an institutional habit.

Let's first be honest about where and how we have failed. Since Independence in 1947, we have ignored the future of children by investing very little on public health and education. We still spend less than 2 per cent of GDP on public health and just about 3.8 per cent of GDP on education. This has resulted in poor human development indicators. Children without quality education and basic amenities like sanitation and healthcare will find it difficult to develop the skills needed for 21st-century livelihoods. We need to substantially step up both quantitatively and qualitatively on these two fronts.

During the recent Bharat Yatra against child sexual abuse, children led the way and became agents of change. They created a mass movement against a horrific social evil that is becoming a moral epidemic in India. In every village, town and city, it was children who came up with stirring words and innovative solutions. It was children who have inspired me to continue this struggle with their courage, clarity and conviction. One powerful symbol has been Kinshu, who was rescued by us from child slavery. He has joined me in all my marches. He is now an engineer.

It was a stirring moment when Manisha, who had been sold multiple times as a sex slave, made a direct and emotional appeal to the Hon'ble President of India, Ram Nath Kovind, who hosted Bharat Yatra marchers at the Rashtrapati Bhavan. Her appeal was simple: Children like her from poor families must not be traded as slaves. In fact, Manisha marched alongside me throughout the Yatra and spoke out loudly against child sexual abuse. The sheer moral power and eloquence of the words spoken by Manisha moved the President visibly. He called victims like her, who have been rehabilitated, as the real builders of a new India.

My optimism is not just because of gestures like this. It is also because of individual stories that never make headlines. Fifteen-year-old Ajay from Mirzapur, Uttar Pradesh was condemned to a life of poverty and illiteracy because his father, who is a driver, was too poor to give him education. Today, he is a gifted and valued student at the Bal Ashram run by us and loves playing cricket.

Whenever I have marched, it is children who have led the way and forced the world to change. In 1998, we organised a Global March against Child Labour. The world was stunned when children marched inside the ILO headquarters in Geneva and demanded their rights. It was children who spoke in powerful cadence when we marched in 2001, demanding that education be made a fundamental right. It is children who have inspired me to do more for them.

You could call them glimpses of a million mutinies. I would call them glimpses of a million opportunities for our children. Our children have the dreams, the talent and the faith to achieve. The most fitting way to celebrate Children's Day is not to indulge in mere rhetoric, but it lies in us to collectively empower our children. They have a future; so does India. The question is: Can we unshackle their dreams?

❑

7

March with Me and Stop Children being Robbed of Childhood

When I first caught word of the announcement that Malala Yousafzai and I would be this year's Nobel Peace Prize recipients, a swirl of joyful emotions overcame me.* As family, friends, staff, members of the media and various well-wishers swarmed my Delhi office, it was as if I'd been transported to the time nearly 50 years ago when I experienced the first truly transformational moment in my life.

The earliest seeds of my struggle to fight for children's rights were planted on my very first day of school. I was just five. As I approached the school entrance, I noticed a boy of my age polishing shoes with his father. "Sir, why isn't your son going to school with the rest of us?" I asked. "We are born to work," was his reply. I really wanted that boy to learn and play with me, so his father's response confused and upset me.

The transformative moment came six years later. The tradition in my town of Vidisha (Madhya Pradesh) on the last day of my school was for everyone to throw away their textbooks. This made no sense to me. Wouldn't the children in the class below us benefit from our textbooks the same as we had — not to mention the cobbler boy and other children who are unable to attend school?

---

* This column was written soon after the author was awarded the Nobel Peace Prize. Here, the author recounts his decades-long struggle to ensure a more dignified and free life for children across the world.

My friend and I rented a vegetable cart and walked around the neighbourhood convincing everyone to put their books in the cart rather than throw them away. I had no idea how people would react, and so I was quite anxious. But as the word of our experiment spread through the village, our cart soon overflowed with books. I was overcome with emotion as we shared the books with those who needed them most. Later that night, tears of joy streamed down my face.

That was the moment when I first realised that change is always possible. It was the moment a new Kailash was born in me.

When the status quo is unjust, we must always challenge it. The real answer to my question to the cobbler boy's father was not that some people are simply born to work but rather that some things in this world are unjust; and none more so than robbing children of their childhood.

From child soldiers to trafficking for labour and sex, from inter-generational bonded labour to girls forbidden to attend school, the list of appalling injustices committed against children is, unfortunately, a long one. In the face of such horrors inflicted upon the most innocent of God's creations, many have asked how I have been able to remain so optimistic. It is because in the 34 years since giving up my career as an electrical engineer to dedicate myself full time to my cause, I have seen tremendous progress. It is also because the soul of humanity itself demands it. If we do not change our ways, I fear we are on a collision course with a suicidal fate where violence triumphs over peace and where extremism triumphs over tolerance.

The same voice that told me over 50 years ago that the little cobbler boy should have been in school playing and learning with me is telling me now that compassion for the world's children can be a unifying force that patches humanity's soul and puts us on the right course again.

When we possess the resources today to end child slavery tomorrow and yet choose not to, this is devastating to the soul of humanity. Every year that we choose to spend more on instruments of destruction than on schools for our children, our collective soul is diminished.

And so it is imperative that the march towards progress moves forward. Let us unite with the children. Let us preserve their innocence. Let us put every last one of them in school. Let us teach them peace, tolerance and courage. Let us protect their fate and in doing so, protect our own.

We cannot continue to let the same forces that divided us during the dawn of civilisation divide us still. And therein lies the hidden power of children — because whether you're a woman from the east or a man from the west, no matter what your religion, political views or anything else are, we can agree that our children are the most innocent and precious of all gifts. All too often we may find themselves struggling for survival and desperately clinging to hope where little is to be found.

And so we must protect them and keep our promises to them.

Progress will come at great cost, as it has already. My colleagues and I once attempted to rescue a group of Nepali girls trafficked and forced to work as circus performers. Not even the cameras from the media that were capturing the unfolding scene were enough to deter the circus owner from pulling a gun and mercilessly beating us.

But we were not deterred either. Brave bystanders huddled around us, carried us to their vehicle and drove us to the hospital. I went on a hunger strike demanding the release of the girls and this was finally granted four days later. As a direct result of this incident, the Indian courts finally banned the use of children as circus performers. You see, change is possible, my friend.

In speaking truth to power, some of my fellow activists have paid the ultimate price. In the name of these courageous martyrs and the millions of children still enslaved and entrapped, I ask you to join me in this march — for courage must always triumph over fear.

❑

8

New Juvenile Justice Law: Well Begun but only Half Done

The barbaric assault on a young woman on December 16, 2012 in New Delhi and the unprecedented public outcry that followed the incident have altered the way our laws and policies view the protection of women from sexual violence. While it is true that court judgements/ amendments of the existing laws will not alter the events that happened that night in New Delhi, the legal changes, if implemented properly, could prevent the recurrence of such incidents.

The Juvenile Justice (Care and Protection of Children) Bill, 2015 was passed in the Rajya Sabha last month and it was heartening to see MPs join hands to debate and pass the new law that aims to recognise new crimes against children — trafficking, organised crime, armed conflict, child marriage, drugs and bonded labour.*

Along with the creation of new policies and institutions, there is also an urgent need to strengthen the existing ones. For example, all those responsible for the care and protection of children in the child welfare committees, juvenile justice boards, the national and state commissions

---

* This column was written as a critique of the Juvenile Justice Bill that was cleared in 2016. Sustained efforts by the author, his colleagues and other activists resulted in a much more humane and effective law being passed in 2017.

for the protection of child rights and in children's homes must be appointed on merit.

They also need to be sensitised and trained on various aspects concerning children, given adequate resources and authority and must be held accountable for their performance. The record of enforcement of the existing JJA (Juvenile Justice Act) has been uninspiring. Whatever little action has happened till now has been thanks to the Supreme Court.

The Centre has allotted ₹ 2,000 per month per child living in children's homes and childcare institutions. This includes food, lodging, education and protection costs. This is very little money and so the quality of care in these institutions leaves much to be desired. This allocation should be increased to at least ₹ 5,000 per month in order to ensure education, development and care of each child. According to several reports, children constitute almost 40 per cent of the population but the government spends only 0.4 per cent of the GDP on them.

There is still much to be done when it comes to improving the standards of rehabilitation. Even reform frameworks are yet to be defined. The incidents of abuse in these children's homes only prove that they must be reformed. In a first step forward, the JJ Bill seeks compulsory registration of children's homes. This will go a long way towards checking trafficking and will assist in the re-unification of missing children with their families. This would also be the first step towards ensuring standardisation of the quality of children homes across the country.

In addition to the existing system of rehabilitation and reformation, the Bill states that if a juvenile between 16-18 years commits a heinous crime, s/he may be tried in a children's court and not by the juvenile justice board. Moreover, they will be tried as an adult only if the board deems necessary. Following this, if the children's court decides, the juvenile may be further sent to a designated 'place of safety' (as defined by the law) for reformation and rehabilitation. In the unlikely scenario of the failure of rehabilitation and reformation, s/he can go to an adult jail after detailed assessment and upon turning 21.

The systems of decision-making in the juvenile justice board on reformation and rehabilitation and education require investments in innovation, open-mindedness, building knowledge and capacity of the enforcement and childcare agencies, transparency, regular monitoring and social audit to ensure its success. The success of the JJ law must not to be measured by the number of juveniles we send to homes or places of safety but by the number of children who are protected, reformed and rehabilitated by them and the number of adults being punished for crimes against children.

Faster mechanisms in order to facilitate proper governance and execution of the law with time-bound procedures are also needed. Notably, the Protection of Children from Sexual Offences Act has a conviction rate of only one per cent and pendency of 95 per cent. Fast-track courts in every district to address heinous crimes against women and children, policy framework for access to justice, witness and victim protection, economic compensation and rehabilitation, and robust forensic science, technology focus and enhanced capability are also much needed at all levels.

The measure of a society and its future lies in the way it treats its children. Our collective frustration over the impunity enjoyed by perpetrators of crimes has resulted in a demand for justice. However, justice is also in ensuring a deterrent for crimes against children; in stepping forward against trafficking, child marriage and child labour; by accepting education and protection for all children as the benchmarks for sustainable development and that all crimes result in responsibility, enough deterrent, ample rehabilitation and reformation. I like to believe that anyone and everyone can be reformed. All we need to do is change the way our children can dream and the way we look at them.

❑

9

Please Spare Our Children

More and more children are being devoured by conflicts across the world. This is a collective global failure.

The wanton killings never seem to stop. A bomb attack on refugees inside their own homeland in Syria led to the ghastly death of 68 children in Aleppo. There were haunting visuals of weeping journalists and aid workers working in vain to save at least some of the babies. In the dystopian nightmare that Syria has become, nobody knows for sure who is responsible for this barbaric assault. A few days before this, about 30 children were slaughtered in a chemical weapons attack. Once again, there is no clinching evidence of who used gas to kill children. More than 17,000 children have died in Syria since civil war erupted five years ago.*

For all citizens of the world who believe in basic humanity, the time has come to demand urgent and immediate intervention. The Security Council of the United Nations has the military power to bring to a halt this unceasing genocide. Perhaps the time has now come to add moral authority to that. At the end of the day, it is all about morality. Saving children and giving them an opportunity to try and build a better future is a scared moral duty of all

* This article poignantly highlights how children become 'collateral damage' in conflict zones. It asks world leaders to come together to protect the millions of children being killed, injured or rendered homeless because of civil wars.

mankind. Scoring diplomatic debating points is fine, but we have crossed the stage of rhetoric. Future generations will never forgive us if the global powers who have the means to stop the genocide do not act now. Who said morality doesn't have the power to impact the powerful.

When I read about these unspeakable horrors, I am reminded of my youth when America was fighting a brutal and bitter war in Vietnam. It is ordinary and patriotic Americans who were revolted and outraged when reports of children being massacred and victimised started filtering through. The My Lai massacre of 1968 where 171 chidren were killed in cold blood shocked an entire generation of young Americans and led to widespread anti-war protests. And when a photo of an eight-year-old naked girl screaming and running for life after she was burnt in a napalm attack was released in 1972, the tide finally turned and morality started prevailing over power. Vietnam was both a shame and a beacon of hope.

But almost fifty years after My Lai, are children safer in regions convulsed by conflicts? It is with a heavy heart that I have to admit that the abuse of helpless children has become even more endemic even as globalisation and technology have led to instant and widespread sharing of atrocities against children. In Nigeria, more than 200 school girls were kidnapped and kept at gun-point for years as sex slaves. There was widespread outrage but most of the girls remained captives. In Pakistan, a few years ago, 150 young boys were butchered by gunmen inside their own school. And each day, we get to know about horror stories of young Yazidi girls being raped and assaulted for weeks on end. Then there are widespread reports of how tens of thousands of these children from conflict zones were being trafficked into lives of bonded labour or forced prostitution. I sometimes feel that we collectively as humanity have abandoned these helpless children.

Of course, this is not to conclude that global institutions have not made efforts to protect children and ensure a better future for them through improved access to education, healthcare and livelihood opportunities. Collective efforts across the world have led to a global ban on child labour and stringent provisions against trafficking. The sustainable development goals of the United Nations have drawn up a clear roadmap till 2030. But is it enough?

The fact is that children continue to be victimised and brutalised. Children constitute one-third of the total population of the world, but account for more than 50 per cent of refugees. In the last 10 years, close to 10 million children have been killed in conflict and more than six million have become physically disabled. It is estimated that 28 million children have become refugees without any hope for a future. Syria and Afghanistan alone accounted for more than 50 per cent of child casualties and refugees in 2015.

Children are never responsible for any wars, conflicts or violence, yet they are its worst sufferers. In these times of extreme unrest, it becomes our collective duty to protect the millions of children who, being the most vulnerable, get caught in the crossfire of bombs, bullets and chemical attacks. I strongly demand the UN Security Council to set up a high-power group to tackle violence against children in situations of conflict, refugee crises, cross-border trafficking and slavery in a time-bound manner.

Fifty years ago, it was My Lai. Today, it is Aleppo. Can we not tug our collective conscience?

❑

10

The Fig Leaf of Marriage

In the 37 years that I have spent fighting for the fundamental rights of children, I have encountered many adversaries, critics and opponents. Perhaps the most formidable and enduring of them have always been symbolised by three simple terms: Customs, traditions and social institutions.* It has been easier to combat in your face bigotry and cruelty than entrenched prejudice masquerading as social science. During the same 37 years, I have received tremendous support from all sections of Indian society. But I must single out the two whose unstinted help and support has helped our movement win many a battle. One is the ordinary Indian citizen who often understands humanity far more deeply than the urban elite; the second is the Indian judiciary, particularly the higher judiciary whose judgements and verdicts have step by step made India a better and safer place for children.

Just a few days ago, the Supreme Court reaffirmed our faith by eliminating a glaring lacunae in our law. In a decisive verdict, the Court has stated that sexual intercourse with a minor amounts to statutory rape even if she is married. In effect, men can no longer cover themselves with the fig leaf of marriage if they have sex with a girl below

* Child marriage is an evil social practice that persists despite numerous efforts by the State as well as civil society. This article argues how the Supreme Court verdict declaring sex with even married minors is a giant step forward.

18 years of age. This verdict finally puts to rest the myriad confusions and contradictions seen in different sets of laws that have been passed in the last decade or so. One such law is the Child Marriage Act of 2006 which stipulates that any marriage of a girl below 18 years of age is illegal and null and void. But vast sections of Indian society remain socially regressive and the law is brazenly flouted. India has 23 million women who were married before they turned 18 and barely a few hundred cases have been registered and prosecuted. The Child Marriage Act was a victory for child rights, but an incomplete one.

A major victory for child rights was achieved in 2012 when POCSO was passed. Section 2(d) of the Act defines a child as a person below 18 years of age. Further, Section 5(n) of the Act explicitly states: "Whoever being a relative of the child through blood or adoption or marriage or guardianship or in foster care or having a domestic relationship with a parent of the child or who is living in the same or shared household with the child, commits penetrative sexual assault on such a child is said to commit aggravated penetrative sexual assault." The Act recommended a sentence of rigorous imprisonment not less than 10 years for such a crime. This was a landmark and a milestone for all of us fighting for child rights as we had seen tens of thousands of child rapists get away with such heinous crimes in the absence of a well-defined law. All of us were hopeful that the new law will send a clear signal that child sexual abuse would not go unpunished.

And then Nirbhaya happened and led to more changes in laws relating to rape and sexual assault. But while the new law did add more stringent provisions and broadened the definition of rape and assault, the law makers also passed an Exception 2 to Section 375, which stated: "Sexual intercourse or sexual acts by a man with his own wife, the wife not being under 15 years of age, is not rape." This went not just against the provisions of POCSO but also contradicted the Child Marriage Act. Many of us approached the Supreme Court to rectify this anomaly and it has once and for all made it clear that sexual intercourse with a person below 18 years amounts to rape, irrespective of marital status.

This is a huge victory for child rights and their protection. Teenaged tribal girls from eastern India are being routinely sold as brides to be sexually exploited in north India. Poor Muslim girls in Hyderabad and some other parts of India are sold as child brides to rich Arabs to be sexually abused. The latest verdict plugs the legal loophole that was being used to continue the sexual exploitation of girls. I have just travelled 11,000 kilometres across 22 states of India on a Bharat Yatra to reawaken India's slumbering conscience on the issue of sexual abuse of children. Verdicts like this go a long way in strengthening our cause.

And laws do prod society to change for better. In 2005, 47 per cent of the marriages in India involved children below 18 years of age. The Child Marriage Act came into being in 2006. Despite half-hearted implementation at the local level, the enactment of the law did have an impact. By 2015, the percentage of marriages involving children below 18 had dropped from 47 per cent to 26 per cent.

I am confident the landmark Supreme Court verdict will lead to an even more significant decline in child marriages. Children are meant to play, to study and dream of bright careers. Marriage is a cruelty inflicted on them. It must stop.

❑

11
The Power of Passion and Dreams

Every successful dream is realised when strong foundations in reality give it strength and resilience. Then again, extraordinary feats are achieved when ordinary people decide to speak out and act decisively. When we launched our non-violent war against child rape, sexual abuse and trafficking from the Vivekananda Rock Memorial in Kanyakumari on September 11 in the form of Bharat Yatra, I was relying on the power of dreams and the power of ordinary people.*

Having travelled 12,000 kilometres across 22 states of India and interacting with tens of thousands of people, I am now confident that we will win this war. I can now dream of an India where our children will be safe from predators and of an India where our loud collective voices sweep away the shackles of silence. Victims have decided to speak out, loudly and clearly. While close to 40 million joined us at various stages of the Yatra, a core team of 300 comprising victims and survivors inspired us all the way through their bravery and resilience. Their voices still ring out like a clarion call, though the Yatra is over. At a university ground packed with 8,000 people, 16-year-old Chanda rose and spoke like a thunderstorm that stunned us all. "So you want to know what happened to me in a public toilet? I will no

---

* This was written soon after the culmination of the historic Bharat Yatra against child sexual abuse and trafficking. It showcases how millions of ordinary Indians decided to speak out loudly against the menace.

longer keep quiet about it. I will no longer live in fear and shame," she declared. It is Chanda and hundreds of victims who marched along with me who are reawakening the slumbering conscience of our society. We refuse to accept an India where children remain unsafe; we refuse to accept an India where children can be abused, raped and killed in schools, inside homes, child care centres, hospitals and in public spaces. We need a moral resurgence where the safety of children becomes a social, psychological and emotional issue that binds all of us. We want the safety of children as a defining political agenda.

The President of India was gracious and generous enough to host us at the culmination of the Yatra during a specially organised function at Rashtrapati Bhavan. My request to him and his government was simple and clear: The time has come to form a National Tribunal for Children with statutory powers to ensure the safety of children. We will continue to struggle for it.

Small gestures can make a big difference. I noticed a frail old man sticking posters at Kanyakumari. When I asked about him, he turned out to be Babaji from Mirzapur in Uttar Pradesh and he had travelled thousands of kilometres to join our march from Kanyakumari without needing any invitation. He had marched with me in 1998 during our Global March against Child Labour. Babaji told me, "How could I not join when I heard you had declared a war against child rape?" In Chennai, a young boy walked up fearlessly and shook hands with me. When I asked his name, he told me that he is called Abdul but will now be Satyarthi. He announced passionately, "Sir, you have given a voice to the anguish and agony of children like me." In Guwahati, thousands of young Indians thronged the streets, marching and singing — all demanding an India that is safer for children.

Equally significant has been the whole-hearted support from senior members of judiciary in every state. In Bengaluru, the Hon'ble Chief Justice of the Karnataka

High Court publicly promised that he and his colleagues will ensure speedy justice in POCSO cases and set up special fast-track courts to handle cases of child abuse. In Maharashtra, the Chief Justice of Mumbai High Court promptly agreed to my demand and announced that special task forces would be set up immediately after a case of child abuse is reported. This task force comprising pediatricians, lawyers, psychological counsellors and police officers would offer immediate legal, medical and psychological help to victims in hospitals. In Andhra Pradesh, Chief Minister N. Chandrababu Naidu along with about three lakh citizens marched with us in Kurnool to support our cause. In Hyderabad, spiritual leaders of all faiths pledged their unstinted support for our cause. In Madhya Pradesh, Chief Minister Shivraj Singh Chauhan promised death penalty for child rapists. Everywhere that we have gone and marched so far, mosques, *gurdwaras*, temples and churches have welcomed us with wide open arms. Spiritual leaders of all faiths have been supporting us all the way.

But this war will not be won till our society changes. It will not be won till false notions of family pride and honour and regressive social norms force victims to live in fear and silence. A bolder and more compassionate society would not have allowed the uncle of a 12-year-old girl to keep raping her till her pregnancy was so advanced that abortion was not an option. Child victims are shamed and abused repeatedly. They are abused first by predators. Then they are shamed by society. Finally, they are abused, shamed and harassed inside court rooms where cases take years to be decided. Isn't it a matter of shame for us that barely 5 per cent of cases under POCSO result in conviction?

Our Bharat Yatra has indeed concluded, but it is also a beginning. It is the beginning of a movement where ordinary Indians take a pledge to demand and fight for the safety of their children. For the safety of all children. India can never be free and never be safe till our children are safe. Let us redeem our moral obligation to them.

❑

12
Trafficking: A Moral and Economic Fight

Ideas have legs. So do human beings. When ideas are chained, we desecrate the very fundamentals of freedom. When human beings are chained, we desecrate the fundamentals of humanity. One of the monumental milestones for mankind is the abolition of slavery and bondage. This single act is proof that society and civilisation have the ability to move forward when it comes to freedom and dignity. But while we have won many decisive wars against slavery and bondage, we haven't succeeded in completely vanquishing this degrading and dehumanising practice.*

As we mark the World Day against Trafficking* in person, let us remind ourselves of some sobering and deeply disturbing facts. According to the International Labour Organisation, more than 21 million people across the world are victims of trafficking. In other words, they are de facto 21st-century slaves. That is more than double the population of Hungary and Bolivia and almost equal to the entire population of Australia. While sexual slavery and forced labour remain the major drivers behind trafficking,

---

* This column was written to commemorate the World Day against Trafficking. It reveals how trafficking has become the largest criminal enterprise in the world and how urgent global steps are needed to tackle this.

shocking new trends have emerged. At least 10 nations have reported that trafficking has been related directly with organ harvesting. This is now a $ 32 billion-a-year business according to the UN. But humanitarian agencies reckon that it has surpassed drugs and arms as the largest criminal business in the world with an annual revenue of $ 150 billion. Women and children constitute 71 per cent of the victims. How can any civilisation allow this atrocity to continue and flourish? Is our commitment to the vulnerable victims a mere parroting of empty slogans?

I recently pointed out in the United States that the line between migration and trafficking is becoming very thin. It has been consistently noticed that the geographical paths and routes of trafficking bear striking resemblance with those of migration. Natural and increasing scale of man-made disasters, particularly armed conflicts and civil wars are creating a whole new generation of refugees who are becoming victims of trafficking gangs. Syria is a stark reminder of this trend. Clearly, law enforcement agencies in developed countries as well as a host of global bodies tasked to check and prevent trafficking need much more coordination and cooperation. This is all the more important because the UN itself has made it clear while laying down the 2030 sustainable development goals that a rise in economic prosperity and equality directly leads to a fall in trafficking. So far, we have seen a lot of rhetoric on this. We now need more action.

India has not been immune to this global scourge. Official data indicates that close to 20,000 women and children were trafficked in India in 2016, but the real numbers could be far higher. More than 1,00,000 children go missing every year. More than half of them are never traced. Most of the untraced children become slaves of begging and prostitution rackets. Since most victims of trafficking belong to poor and marginalised families, hardly anyone, including police personnel, pay much attention to these tens of thousands of family tragedies. But a historic Supreme Court judgement of 2013 based on a petition by our movement 'Bachpan Bachao Andolan' has prodded authorities to pay more attention to this menace. Yet, trafficking and slavery continue to flourish in India.

And the stories are tragic. We had rescued 13-year-old Malvika (name changed) from Gurgaon. She was trafficked from a village in West Bengal with promises of good wages. Her life was hell after that. In two consecutive homes where Malvika was working as a domestic help, she was like a slave with the employers routinely beating her. In both the houses, she was raped repeatedly by drivers. Malvika is lucky that she was rescued and is back with her family. Hundreds of thousands of victims like her have not been as lucky. What can we do in India to stop the barbarity against young girls like Malvika?

For starters, we need a strong law against trafficking. Despite endless debates and repeated pleas by civil society groups, stringent anti-trafficking laws have not been passed by the Parliament, nor have state governments taken meaningful measures to stop this atrocity. It took almost 19 years for India to ratify the ILO conventions that prohibit the worst forms of child labour. Let us not drive hundreds of thousands of innocent children into cruel and miserable lives of slavery by indulging in such unforgivable delays. The Woman and Child Development Ministry has taken steps to tackle trafficking. But real action against the criminals and the gangs will come when police personnel and other law enforcement agencies get seriously involved. We, as citizens, too need to play a more proactive role by refusing to keep our eyes and ears closed. We must protest and report cases of suspected trafficking victims in our neighbourhoods. That is a moral imperative.

Equally important is the need to target the economic roots behind trafficking. In our 37 years of movement, we have rescued more than 85,000 children across India who were victims of bonded labour and slavery. Almost all the children came from extremely poor families. It is states like West Bengal, Jharkhand, Assam and Odisha that still witness extreme poverty that report the most cases of trafficking.

Apart from vastly improved awareness and law enforcement, what India needs to deal with trafficking and slavery is economic opportunities. When poor families earn enough to feed themselves, they become less vulnerable to criminal gangs. When incomes of poor families improve, their children go to school instead of seeking work. When children go to school, their chances of being trafficked and sold into slavery diminishes dramatically.

For 70 years or so, India has not ensured economic security for a large number of its citizens.

The menace of trafficking will remain as long as families remain desperately poor. Of what help is India becoming an economic superpower if hundreds of millions remain in poverty with their children vulnerable to predatory traffickers?

❑

13
Why Education is the Last Frontier

There is a frequently used old proverb that says: Give a man a fish and he will eat for a day; teach him how to fish and he will eat for a lifetime. Let me change this a little: Give a girl a morsel and she will eat for a day; give her a quality education and she will feed a few generations. We are living in exciting times when science and technology are opening up electrifying new possibilities.*

The mapping of the human DNA and biotechnology are opening doors that were earlier believed to be permanently shut. A small hand-held device can now hold, transmit and share knowledge that legions of priests in an earlier era could never dream of. And yet, amidst all this excitement of new discoveries and new conquests, we face a stark and brutal reality — more than 170 million children across the world are denied the fundamental right to education because they are compelled to toil as child labour. A key SD (Sustainable Development) goal of the United Nations is education for all by 2030. The moral and economic challenge that confronts us now is the one of bringing down the shameful number of 170 million to as close to zero as possible in one generation of sustained effort. Indeed, there is a magic wand that can be waved – and that is access to education for all children.

* In this analytical piece, the author argues how education is the most powerful tool not just to fight child labour, but also to ensure a better future for all children as well as the countries in which they live.

Education has the power not only to transform an individual, but entire communities and nations. Any society that claims to be civilised would ensure that every child, no matter from what background, enjoys access to education. It is education that empowers and provides children the means and the freedom to chase their dreams. Moral dimensions matter as does simple economics. Let's take the example of ethnic Indian Americans in the United States to illustrate this powerful point. The per capita income of India is still below $ 2,000 a year. But, in America, Indians are the richest ethnic community with a median income of more than $ 100,000 a year. That is simply because ethnic Indians are the most highly educated community in America. That is the transformative power of education.

One major reason why India is a laggard and persistently poor performer in terms of human development indicators as well as economic growth is education, or the lack of this as a fundamental right. Till the 1960s, India reported higher per capita incomes than almost all Asian counterparts excluding Japan. Today, those countries, including China are far ahead of India in terms of economic prosperity. One key reason is that literacy rate in those countries is well above 90 per cent while we are still struggling with a literacy rate of about 70 per cent in India. A United Nations study demonstrates that every year of additional education leads to an improvement of almost 0.40 per cent in GDP growth rate.

The Bal Mitra Gram concept promoted by us in many states has created many inspirational stories. One of them is 20-year-old Fatima, who belongs to small and deeply conservative Muslim-dominated village in Meerut district of western Uttar Pradesh. Like millions before her, Fatima faced a life of early marriage and the end of dreams. But when the young girl was made a leader of a Bal Panchayat more than 10 years ago, she discovered a new world of opportunities. She became the second girl from her village to pursue a graduate degree in Meerut. There are 11 more girls like her from the village doing the same now. Fatima mentors and provides free tuitions to more than 100 children in her village of which about 50 are girls. And she is determined to become an IAS officer. India needs millions of more inspirations like Fatima.

We are and will always remain deeply committed to universal access to education for children and the elimination of child labour. Both are directly interlinked. But this is just what we can achieve in a vast nation like India with our limited resources. Education, like health, remains universally recognised as a public good and no State can absolve itself from the moral duty of investing in this public good. The private sector cannot be the solution. Every nation in the world that has achieved very high literacy rate has benefitted from massive and sustained public investment in education. This holds good even for the so-called capitalist countries in Western Europe and North America.

Unfortunately, the Indian State seems to have abdicated this responsibility for decades. To be sure, welfare schemes like Mid-Day Meals and NREGA have led to a big rise in school enrolment. And policies like Right to Education have offered poor children a window of opportunity in private schools. But it is simply not enough. Recent data suggests that almost 50 per cent of children in India still drop out after primary school. And the figure rises to 75 per cent after secondary school. To befit with, investment in education as a share of GDP must be doubled from the current level of about 3 per cent.

That would be a good beginning. But it would just be a beginning.

❑

14

Why I am Marching Again

Freedom never comes to us as a gift-wrapped package. Freedom from fear is a struggle that is a relentless quest for courage and compassion. We live in times when we constantly engage in loud debates on a whole range of issues. But I have noticed how our collective conspiracy of silence becomes deafening when it comes to our most precious assets — our children. Over the last few months, I have met dozens of young innocent children who have been ravaged by monsters in acts of sexual barbarity. I have met family members of young children who have been brutally raped and murdered. I have tried my best to comfort parents who have lost their children to trafficking gangs. Their pain and sorrow are not just an indictment of our society, but they have also made me realise that my life-long quest for child rights remains an unfinished struggle.*

That is why, I have decided to march again. For me and for the children of India, this march is nothing short of a declaration of war against child sexual abuse and trafficking. Silence on this issue is no longer acceptable. It would amount to cowardice. I refuse to accept that predators can roam free and fearless while victims live in fear. I am marching to give a voice to these helpless victims

---

* This column was written soon after the author announced the Bharat Yatra against child sexual abuse and trafficking. It exhorts Indians to break the conspiracy of silence that envelops this crime against humanity.

and to reawaken the slumbering conscience of our nation. Child sexual abuse must stop.

I appeal to all of you to join me in this historic march and become the voice of children. The Bharat Yatra will be launched from Kanyakumari on September 11, 2017 and move towards Delhi. Hundreds of thousands of ordinary Indians like you and me have pledged support and will be joining different legs of the Yatra from Srinagar in the north to Guwahati in the east to Ahmedabad in the west. This march will be a collective and resounding voice opposing violence against children.

Four years ago, five-year-old Gudiya was sexually abused in the most inhuman manner by perverts near her house. She is still recovering. Her father has pledged support to our movement against child sexual abuse. Some weeks ago, 16-year-old Gudiya, who lived near Shimla, was gangraped and murdered on her way back from school. Her father is a shattered man. But he wants to do anything he can to stop other young girls from becoming victims like his daughter. He is with me in this march.

The sad and harsh reality is that sexual abuse of children is becoming a moral epidemic in this country. The victims can come from poverty-stricken slums to affluent-gated communities. The predators are drivers, teachers, neighbours and close relatives. This sinister fear has gripped parents across the country; they worry when children are late in reaching home. This fear has to be erased. Official data states that close to 50 children are sexually abused every day in this country. In reality, the number would be far higher as in a majority of cases where relatives become predators, parents don't report the crime for fear of social stigma. I am marching to persuade parents to speak out loudly and clearly even if rapists happen to be their relatives. Children are far more valuable than sham notions of social respect and family pride.

Another sad and harsh reality is that laws are not proving to be enough of a deterrence, despite POCSO being enacted in 2012. In Delhi, it will take 12 years to clear the pending cases of child sexual abuse. It will take more than 20 years in Maharashtra and a shocking 40 years in Gujarat. Justice delayed is not just justice denied; it is also justice raped and murdered. My march is to protest against this.

I have spent more than 36 years fighting for child rights. I have undertaken many Yatras. In almost all cases, I have initially encountered cynicism, apathy and even downright hostility for revealing ugly realities of our society. But then, when victims have gathered courage to speak out and when ordinary citizens have lent their support, social attitudes have changed. Almost the whole of India was sceptical when I launched a Yatra from Bihar to Delhi to protest against child labour in 1993. Almost the whole world was cynical when we organised the Global March against Child Labour in 1998. Child labour was considered to be a normal practice. But when dozens of young children marched with me inside the headquarters of International Labour Organisation in Geneva and spoke out, the world took notice. Within a year, the ILO passed a convention that made the worst firms of child labour illegal. Small voices can have a mighty impact.

We urgently need a collection of small voices against child sexual abuse and trafficking. I have no doubt that the Bharat Yatra will persuade and provoke India to rise in revolt against this social evil. If you and I don't demand safety for our children, then who will?

❑

15

Seven Reasons Why We must March Against Child Rape

The rape of children, their abuse and the manner in which they are being trafficked is no longer just a law and order problem; it seems to be a moral epidemic that has gripped our society and threatens to destroy our moral foundations. I have embarked on a gruelling Bharat Yatra that was launched from Kanyakumari on September 11, 2017.* For me, the Yatra is a declaration of war against child rape. Beyond the rhetoric, here are some reasons why you must join the march.

Because Children Need Freedom: We have been celebrating 70 years of Indian Independence. There is much to celebrate, no doubt, but do our children enjoy freedom? They are increasingly unsafe inside their own homes, in schools and in other public places. Parents panic when children are late because of the widespread extent of child sexual abuse and violence. India can only be truly free when children are free from fear.

Because Crime must not Pay: No civilised society allows criminals to get away. The punishment is particularly harsh when children become victims because they are the most vulnerable and defenceless. And yet we have a situation in

---

* Soon after the author announced the Bharat Yatra, many asked him to specify the real reasons behind the march and why the youth should join. In this piece, the author lists seven compelling reasons for young Indians to join him.

India where a majority of minsters who brutalise children manage to escape justice. The conviction rate in child sexual abuse cases is just about 5 per cent. In some states, it will take 40 years to clear the backlog of child rape cases. This can only encourage criminals to act more brazenly.

Because Children are Beyond Ideology and Identity: India is witnessing fierce ideological battles and seems besieged with divisive identity politics. Anger, intolerance and intemperate language seem to have become the norm. But there is one issue where all ideologies, all religions and all identities converge — it is the safety of children. This is one issue where there can be no divisive debate. The safety of children is paramount and the Bharat Yatra is a powerful message to all Indians to give up their differences for once and stand united on this issue.

Because Children Need Education: Tens of thousands of children continue to be trafficked every year, particularly from poor regions in eastern India. Some are sold as child brides; many are sold as sex slaves and many more are lured by 'placement agencies' to become de facto slave labour in upper middle-class homes in big cities. Each one of them is deprived of a fundamental right which is access to education. We must march to demand that every child gets her fundamental right.

Because Children Need Our Support, not Silence: We have allowed the moral epidemic of child abuse to spread because we have chosen to remain silent. Our silence encourages more violence. Criminals take advantage of our silence. The time has come to break this conspiracy of silence and raise our collective voices against this evil. The Bharat Yatra is giving a voice to the hitherto silent victims and their families. That is why me must add our voice.

Because Children Matter more than Honour: We have a very warped and twisted sense of family honour and pride. In a majority of cases of child sexual abuse, the criminals are either relatives or people known to the victims, like school teachers and neighbours. When children get abused, the matter is often hushed up because of a perverted sense of family honour. We often fear that disclosure will shame the victims. It is the rapist who needs to be shamed, not the victim. It is the rapist who needs a social boycott, not the victim. It is time we change our social norms. The Bharat Yatra seeks this kind of social reawakening.

Because Children are Our Future: There is frequent talk of how India is enjoying a demographic dividend as it has the largest number of children on this planet. We keep boasting as to how our children will make India a superpower in the coming decades, but that promise is yet to be fulfilled. And it won't be fulfilled if our children are not safe and do not have access to quality education. If we want our children to redeem our future, let's march for them.

❑

16

Child Labour Fuelling Black Money

Civil society campaigns revolving around corruption and black money have not only eclipsed many fundamental issues confronting the common people of the country but have also become so emotional that pertinent aspects of genesis of these evils have been largely ignored. Illegal employment of children has emerged as a huge source of illicit earnings and corruption.* According to the Census of India 2001, 1.27 crore children were working in various sectors across the country while the non-government organisations estimate the number of child labourers at six crore or nearly 6 per cent of the total population of India.

In spite of the ambiguity in numbers, one thing is evident—children are employed not just because of parental poverty, illiteracy, ignorance, failure of development and education programmes, but quite essentially due to the fact that employers benefit immensely from child labour as children come across as the cheapest option, sometimes even for free. No factory, mine, or workshop owner dares to admit about employing children in their premises against pittance or no wage at all. They normally misappropriate their books of account and show a substantial amount of wage component factored into the production cost. This

---

* In this analytical piece, the author argues how child labour plays a major role in creating and sustaining black money. It points out how existing laws have not acted as a deterrent for offenders.

gap is the real issue. The presence of large number of child labourers in the country indicates unabated corruption and black money.

All work that is done by child labourers and the income thus generated goes unaccounted in a country's economy. Studies reveal that these six crore children assumingly work for approximately 200 days in a year at an average cost of ₹ 15 per child per day. This amounts to ₹ 18,000 crores in one year. Now, these six crore child labourers when substituted with six crores adult labourers would earn ₹ 1,38,000 crores at minimal rate of an average floor wage of ₹ 115 per day per labourer for 200 days. This difference in the total earnings between the two scenarios works out to ₹ 1,20,000 crores — which is solely a pool of black money.

This is a straight profit of ₹ 1,20,000 crore, which is a significant loss to the economy. The employer(s) should have legally and ideally paid this sum to the worker(s) but the employer(s) instead choose to employ docile, underpaid and overworked child labourers.

Part of this black money generated by employing child labour is used in bribing the law enforcement agencies and politicians. This is chronic corruption. This, in turn, leads to lax implementation of laws, i.e. poor or no inspection of the work premises, letting the employers scott free with little or no penalties at all, etc. This subsequently propels child labour creating an unscrupulous vicious circle between child labour, black money and corruption.

In response to a question in the Parliament, the government admitted that only 9 per cent of employers of child labourers have so far been convicted since 2007. This conviction is in the form of a fine only. In spite of one year to three years' imprisonment provisions in the laws related to Child Labour and Bonded Labour, unsurprisingly not even a single errant employer has been jailed so far.

The influence of black money generated through child labour is visible in those areas where child labour is endemic. Despite the large-scale production and even export of certain goods, these areas remain shockingly underdeveloped. In Mirzapur-Bhadohi belt of U.P. where the multi-million dollar carpet industry is concentrated, why is it that no major industrial development has been encouraged or agricultural reforms undertaken so far? Adult migration in search of livelihood to other cities is quite high as well.

Similarly, in Sivakasi, Tamil Nadu, a shocking revelation of jeopardising a large irrigation project by the local politicians came into limelight a few years ago. The reason was obvious. When significant development takes place in an area, per capita income should accordingly increase and villagers should have no reason to send their children to work in the fire-cracker or match-work industries. Tirupur in Tamil Nadu is popularly unpopular for employing large number of child labourers in its knitwear industry. Noyyal River in the city has turned completely toxic because of the industrial waste and effluents.

Although a more in-depth research is needed to further explain how the rightful wages of workers are plundered to create black money, one thing that has been proved and established is, 'child labour is injurious to the health of the economy'. Apart from gathering knowledge and corroborating evidence, this grave situation calls for devising new and efficient ways to act politically, administratively and legally against employers of child labourers in a different manner. Conventionally, such employers are prosecuted only under the provisions of labour or juvenile laws, but in the light of black money, they must be inclusively booked under finance and tax-related crimes as well.

❑

17

Child Rights' Protection: The Triangular Paradigm

For the first time, Ministers of Labour and Education, civil society groups, donors and top officials of UNESCO, ILO, UNICEF, World Bank and other organisations discussed at a round-table conference on November 13 in New Delhi as to how they could work in unison in achieving Education For All (EFA) and combating child labour within a broader poverty reduction strategy in line with the Millennium Development Goals. This followed the third annual High Level Group (HLG) meeting on Education For All on November 11-12, organised by UNESCO and hosted by the Government of India. At this critical round table, we tried to focus on the triangular paradigm on child rights' protection.*

The three key processes affecting the future of the world, in particular our children, are poverty alleviation, elimination of child labour and Education For All. They are gaining more concrete shape within the framework of Millennium Development Goals (MDGs) and poverty reduction strategies, Dakar goals to ensure EFA by 2015 by all the countries in eliminating the worst forms of child labour through implementation of ILO Conventions 182 and

* In this reasoned write up, the author argues how poverty alleviation, elimination of child labour and universal education can lead to a more humane and just world order.

138. But my serious concern has always been the ideological, political and practical disjoint between the three processes.

Cheapest Workforce

It is a well-researched truth that there exists a vicious cycle of poverty and child labour as well as illiteracy and child labour. Each of these combinations has a cause and consequence effect simultaneously. Again, in most countries, we see a clear parallel between child labour and adult unemployment. Studies reveal that adults are unable to find jobs for even 100 days in a year, and if at all they do find one, their legal minimum wages are denied. Being the cheapest and the most vulnerable workforce, children are preferred over adults, resulting in the compromise on low wages or joblessness of the latter.

India, with the largest number of child labourers, has at least 60 million working children and an equal number of unemployed adults. The gross earning of all these children amounts to ₹ 600 million a day ($ 13 million a day). If the adults had been working in their place, they would have been earning at least five times that of these children ($ 65 million a day). At the end of the day, most of these children remain uneducated and unskilled. They have no bargaining power, fall prey to different health hazards, thereby losing vital organs in accidents, and remain sick or handicapped for the rest of their lives. More significantly, their mental development, self-esteem and entrepreneurship remain stymied and they are forced to lead a life of abject poverty.

Education and elimination of child labour are inextricably linked. Education is a key element in preventing child labour. The route to power, social justice, gender equity, decentralisation, effective democracy, good governance and prosperity has to be through classrooms and schools. Though most countries are genuine on the issue of elimination of child labour, there is a lack of coordination in their efforts. The world over, ministries responsible for the elimination of child labour and those responsible for quality education have little or no connection with each other. As for the Finance Ministry — the most powerful and responsible for issues concerning economic growth — it lacks adequate understanding of child labour issues and education as prerequisites to development.

Thus, the efforts made for poverty reduction in most countries do not have strong linkages with Education For All. And most of the developing countries are not prepared to spend even 2 per cent of the income on children's education. At the 2000 World Education Forum in Dakar, 181 countries drafted the Dakar Framework for Action, which set out clear goals such as ensuring education for all children by 2015, eliminating gender disparities in primary and secondary education by 2005 and improving all aspects of the quality of education. Each country is supposed to make concrete and time-bound national action plans to achieve the EFA goals by 2015.

But we cannot achieve this goal unless we ensure the elimination of child labour and make basic education truly free. The cost of textbooks, uniforms and stationery is unaffordable for the poor. Thus, the exorbitant cost of education keeps many children out of school and increases the possibility of the children remaining in hazardous work. How can one ensure enrolment and, more importantly, the retention of children in primary and secondary classes unless a strong effort is made for child labour elimination? Why would a child go for expensive education when he or she is getting an alternative in earning? Why would the illiterate and poor parents not send their children to work against schooling? There is a serious dearth of basic thinking in this direction.

Multi-dimensional Approach

Again, both child labour and education are linked to poverty. Unfortunately, poverty alleviation programmes in most countries do not have strong linkages with education and child labour. As for the projects on child labour undertaken by civil society organisations and government institutions, the vision is narrow. They do not analyse and link them with the broader context of economic environment in families and communities, poverty-related policies, the existing development paradigms and the process of liberalisation, privatisation and globalisation. In this situation, a long-lasting solution to the birth and perpetuation of child labour cannot be ascertained. A multi-dimensional approach consisting of awareness building and consciousness raising, community participation, alternative and viable social and economic rehabilitation, and enforcement of national and international legal instruments in relation to children and other similar plans, is needed for linking child labour with overall poverty-alleviation strategies.

In relation to multilateral and bilateral aid and debt loan, the developing countries are supposed to make the Poverty Reduction Strategy Papers (PRSPs) and country plans. Ironically, child labour eradication does not figure in PRSPs of any country. The challenge raised by the problem of child labour emphasises the need to address the issue within a wider framework of poverty reduction. It also makes it crucial to strengthen the cooperation and coordination among stakeholders in the international community, including the donor countries and international organisations, as reflected in the Oslo Agenda for Action, unanimously adopted at the 1997 International Conference on Child Labour.

With regard to development programmes, the phenomenon is 'top-down', starting with inter-governmental organisations to local self-governance. Among many, three processes in the development arena are definitely significant First, there is the poverty-alleviation programme linked with MDGs, facilitated by the World Bank and UNDP.

The World Bank is also leading the Fast Track Initiative for EFA, facilitating additional resource mobilisation to fill the financing gaps for countries engaged in child labour eradication. The second one is EFA with UNESCO as the lead agency. UNICEF is also spearheading a specific programme on girls' education initiative. The third one concerns the elimination of the worst forms of child labour under the auspices of ILO. These agencies are dealing with different sets of departments, ministries and civil society organisations. But coordination, collaboration and integration among the departments are rare. I strongly feel that a triangular relationship between poverty alleviation, elimination of child labour and 'Education for All' should be built at all levels — local, national and international.

Under the circumstances, we have decided to work not only for the creation of the triangular development paradigm but also to translate it into action. We strongly feel that there is a need for collaboration and coordination among the donor countries, UN agencies and ministries of different departments.

❑

18

Development Destitution

Development is the buzzword today. There is no dearth of information on modern development paradigms, policies and effects across the globe. The materialistic age of development has been converted into a market-driven digital age, where the humane component in terms of feelings and external relationships is being crystallised in digits, powered with data and information. The fate of mankind is being determined by information, speed and a profit motive.*

Ancient Indian visionaries, the *rishis*, perceived human development as that wherein all were benefited, so they could live without fear and pain. All would earn for all and the benefits would be shared. Clearly, the emphasis was on 'all' rather than the 'self'. Ironically, modern-day development is defined, executed and benefited by a few who control the powers of the state, wealth and sophisticated knowledge. The blind race towards increased economic growth; per capita income and per capita energy consumption is resulting in irreparable human and ecological loss. As I said earlier, the ones who possess power benefit the most, and who are the losers? None other than the children belonging to economically, socially and

---

* In this critique, the author argues how and why excessive focus on traditional markers and measures of development have ignored both human suffering as well as opportunities to create a sustainable world.

sometimes politically excluded communities in the southern hemisphere and, in a few instances, in the North as well.

Globally, there are certain accepted parameters for assessing development, and just to get a fair idea of where we stand, I'd like to share the following facts. Nearly 900 million people go to bed hungry everyday. One billion people have a per capita income of less that $ 1, and half of the world's population earns less than $ 2 a day. There are nearly one billion illiterate people in the world and the same numbers do not have access to safe drinking water. There are around 40 million victims of HIV/AIDS in the world and 246 million child labourers across the globe, two-thirds of them are engaged under most intolerable conditions similar to slavery. These figures are not merely numbers but comment on the so-called 'development' that we have achieved so far, and provokes us to take a critical look at 'development' as we understand it today.

The biggest critique of development as it has progressed over the years has been the fact that development policies and programmes have been and continue to be planned and implemented in a completely undemocratic and non-participatory manner. Development and its benefits are meant for the country as a whole and its citizens in particular, but what is seen in most instances is that while certain sections of society benefit from these policies and programmes, there are certain sections that are completely left out. Development needs to be inclusive of all, more so, of those groups who are of higher vulnerability. It is fairly simple to understand if the programmes have failed to address the very basic issues of hunger, disease and illiteracy, then they have not been designed for all. The ruling elite with whom the decision-making powers lie, use their positions to forward their own cause, leaving a gaping hole in between, through which millions fall each year. A participatory process of development would mean to set in place a process through which stakeholders influence and share control over priority-setting, policy-making, resource allocations and access to public goods and services.

Another problem has been that of short-sighted development programmes or goals, which have obviously meant that any progress made will not be sustainable. To have vision and anticipate development needs 20 or even 50 years hence to make a programme sustainable. What has now happened is that a flurry of 'quick-fix' programmes has led to serious environmental damage and ecological imbalance. In the haste for growth, which is economically oriented, we have forgotten to conserve our very limited reserves of natural resources. We need to preserve our natural resources and ecosystems on which we and our future generations depend. Development should include economic growth with environmental protection and each should reinforce the other.

Other problems that arise due to short-sightedness are those of migration and displacement of people. Largely, strengthening industry or infrastructure is prioritised in development programmes rather than agriculture or small-scale industries, leading to inadequate economic opportunities in places of origin. What happens in the process has a two-fold effect. On the one hand, it is leading to a decline in traditional forms of livelihood; as these are not upgraded and made contemporary to fit in with the changing needs which make them redundant and, therefore, do not present a viable option of livelihood for people. The second is that of large-scale labour force migration. In the process, complex problems related to migrant workers, urban slum settlements with inadequate facilities for education, health and employment arise, leading to a whole new cycle of poverty. Trafficking also becomes a major issue in these circumstances, as women and children being vulnerable and worst affected by problems of displacement are easily victimised. We need to understand that an increase in the well-being of the poor will take place only with the protection and enhancement of their environmental, social and skill-related assets, and any development plans made need to be futuristic and keeping these factors in mind.

Let me give you a first-hand instance of the cost of so-called development. A group of 'Bachpan Bachao Andolan' activists and other supporters were informed by social activists that many labourers from Chhattisgarh were being kept in captivity as bonded labourers for building a hotel in Connaught Place. Their children were also being forced to work along with their parents. While looking into this incident, we came across a woman in dire need of treatment and medication. She had been working at the construction site, carrying bricks on her head upto 10 or 11 storeys in an advanced stage of pregnancy. She had an accident at the site while working, which resulted in an immediate miscarriage of the baby. She was seriously ill but nobody, including the contractor, had bothered to attend to her. The woman had earlier lost her husband while working at the same construction site in another accident. However, she did not receive any additional support from the contractor. This case is a clear example of how people of marginalised groups, especially women and children, are victimised.

Development today has become largely materialistic in nature, with the rich focussing on getting richer and countries measuring their growth by their GDP. Why is it that indicators pertaining to education and health for economically and socially excluded segments of society are not considered as important and the governments do not see these areas of human potential development as critical? The fact that this growth might not be, and, in most cases, is not a mirror of the entire population in a country is conveniently forgotten. A good example is that of Andhra Pradesh state in India. While a former Chief Minister was being lauded as one of the most forward-thinking leaders of the nation, a visionary who was taking his state to new heights in terms of technology and growth, thousands of farmers in the same state were quietly putting an end to their lives. In a country like India, which is primarily an agrarian economy, farmers ending their lives in despair due to poverty shows nothing but apathy of the ruling class towards them. And though I give this example, the same is true for most of the developing and developed economies across the world.

Unfortunately, the biggest victims of such skewed development are invariably children. The vicious cycle of poverty, illiteracy and child labour is one that millions of children are unable to break free from. In India itself, there are several cases of the presence of child labour, whose benefits are reaped by big companies at the cost of the health, education and physical and mental development of these children. Several cases of child abuse and exploitation have been brought to light through the efforts of civil society organisations, human rights groups and other social workers. Some of these children have been released from bondage with the support of the National Human Rights Commission. But several cases still exist where children are working in stone quarries, in brick kilns, cottage industries and even in other hazardous occupations. Domestic child labour, one of the worst forms of child slavery, is on the rise in cities and is mostly invisible. Most of such children belong to families who are displaced or have migrated, underemployed or underpaid, are landless or have lost their traditional source of livelihood, development destitutes or are surviving on the fringes of development. These are problems that exist the world over.

It is often seen that in those areas where land reforms have not been implemented, child labour has increased. This is primarily due to the unequal land holdings that exist and it is the children whose parents do not own land that are forced into child labour. Similarly, in those areas, where minimum wages are not guaranteed, the incidence of child labour is high. Looking at some of the fallouts of development, there are many areas which have suffered serious ecological damages, such as deforestation in the name of construction of highways or dams. Here too, children are the worst affected by the displacement that is caused. The adults, having to give up their traditional source of livelihood, send the children out to work, who are forced to give up their education and support the families. Bihar, for instance, has been seeing terrible floods for the last couple of years and hundreds of families are displaced due to this and many children are orphaned, leaving them in an extremely vulnerable position susceptible to exploitation. Sometimes, these so-called natural disasters, like drought and floods, are actually man-made, brought about by anti-people or anti-nature 'development'-oriented construction.

Tribals and Dalits are perhaps the most vulnerable groups, especially the children and women from these communities. Forest policies, in an effort to keep up with global trends, end up destroying their natural habitat and means of livelihood. Women and children, especially girls, are the worst affected because the responsibility for domestic chores rests with them and they are forced to travel long distances and endure many hardships to fetch water and wood for fuel as well as graze their cattle, which becomes a big obstacle in their schooling.

Any adverse effect of development we see affects children and puts a halt to them exercising their basic rights. Development does not just mean physical development but holistic development of the child, which must ensure that they are able to access all their rights. The perspective of development should be far-sighted and child-centred and the aim should be preservation of ecology, culture, physical environment and equity in sharing the fruits of development. If development policies are framed keeping children in mind, they automatically move away from being short-term objectives and gains to being long-term visions and goals. Development policies must prioritise children's education, investment on their health and investment on social security. It is the responsibility of the state to provide these investments.

Let us take the example of agricultural trade as a case in point of structural deficit. Agriculture is often the economic driving force in the developing countries. However, significant agricultural subsidies provided by developed countries make it impossible for farmers of the developing countries to offer competitive pricing of their products, thereby forcing them to remain in conditions of poverty. We need to ensure that globalisation allows developing countries to enhance their skills and capacity to participate in the global marketplace on an equal footing, so that they can maximise their opportunities in the global agricultural marketplace. Issues related to land ownership and its inequitable distribution, minimum wages and the inability of people to have access to even their basic minimum due legal structures, and the fact that it is only the rich who are able to fight for their rights, reflect the structural deficits that globalisation perpetuates.

Globalisation is furthering a world integrated into a single capitalist mode which is trans-national, rather than national and international in character. It includes the trans-nationalisation of classes and the accelerated division of all humanity into just two classes — global capitalists and global labour. Globalisation, therefore, has profound consequences for each nation of the world system. Productive structures in each nation are reorganised keeping in mind the new international division of labour, characterised by the concentration or polarisation of finances, services, technology and knowledge in the North, and the labour-intensive phases of globalised production in the South. The result is a very distinct polarisation of the world. Politically too, power is seen to be concentrated in one, or maybe a group of countries and this basically is a manifestation of their economic powers, and the results are clearly visible in the invasion of Iraq by America.

The homogenisation of culture which is taking place is destroying the diversity of culture, traditional values and systems. It affects lifestyles, livelihood patterns, agriculture and even food habits. Globalisation has entered and affected almost all aspects of our lives and we need to find a way to ensure that its benefits accrue to all sections of society. The time has come for all well-meaning and educated people to come together in a unified force and demystify knowledge and take it to the masses. At present, no synergised efforts are being made in the direction of development. To fulfil our objectives, we have to form coalitions and develop alliance-building processes to promote the cause of children and marginalised groups in a systematic manner. Their problems have to be addressed in totality and cannot be resolved in isolation.

❑

19

A Child-Friendly World within Our Reach

By conferring the Nobel Prize on Malala and I, the Nobel Committee has recognised one of the most pressing, yet neglected issues of our times. Millions of children still remain invisible, voiceless and unheard. During the last few weeks, their trauma has got unprecedented attention from the law-makers, judiciary and civil society not only in India, but also worldwide.*

Childhood protected and nurtured will yield superior global human capital, while wasted childhood will erode all prospects of a promising tomorrow. Our tomorrow would be as good or as bad as how and what we do about our children today!!!

It is impossible to script global growth leaving behind those 168 million children across the world, who are losing their precious childhood to child labour, out of which 85 million are in hazardous occupations that leave them scarred for life, completely dilapidating their physical, cognitive, moral and social well-being, besides denying their universal right to education. What can be expected of a child who does not get education, continues to do repetitive unskilful tasks and grows up into an adult without any

---

* In this column, the author lists out the major policy changes that must be made to create a world order that respects the dream, dignity and safety of all children across the world.

value-addition? These child labourers inadvertently enter the vicious circle of illiteracy, poverty and child labour, which I term as the 'triangular paradigm'. Thus, child labour and poverty are both cause and consequence of each other. It is impossible to eliminate one without eliminating the other. Look at the painful paradox that while there are 168 million child labourers the world over, there are around 200 million adults worldwide who are jobless. They are the very parents of these child labourers. It won't be an exaggeration to say that child labour is the biggest travesty and scandal of our times.

No prizes for guessing that child labourers are preferred over adults because they are docile, they do not demand minimum wages, they cannot unionise, they work for endless hours as slaves and, at times, fall easy victims of sexual exploitation at the hands of their employers. Today child labourers can be found from farms to mines and factories to homes. Therefore, child labour is as much an issue in the developed countries as it is in the developing countries. Denial of education and freedom is violence against children.

The battle against child labour can only be won by the weapons of six Es — (i) Education; (ii) Employability; (iii) Entrepreneurship; (iv) Efficiency; (v) Equity; and (vi) Ethics.

I cannot emphasise enough the importance of education that gives meaning and direction to life. Education is a perfect antidote for child labour. Children at school form the very foundation of a sustainable and prosperous society. It has been proved beyond reasonable doubts that a single year of primary school increases the wages people earn later in life by 5-15 per cent for boys and even more for girls. For each additional year of secondary school, an individual's wages increase by 15-25 per cent. Furthermore, no country has ever achieved continuous and rapid economic growth without first having at least 40 per cent of its adults able to read and write.

The second weapon of employability is no less important and should be seen as a logical culmination of the global education system coupled with an eclectic balance of vocational and life skills. Education that cannot guarantee employment is very much like a boat without a rudder. Unemployment fuels economic instability and intolerance that can send the youth amok.

Thirdly, entrepreneurship is at the helm of job creation for adults and is an important element for accomplishing a decent work agenda. Entrepreneurship in fact is the prime mover of the global economy.

As an electrical engineer, I draw a clear analogy between minimising transmission loss and increasing the efficiency proportionately. Governments world over will have to be efficient in creating child-friendly policies with a sense of utmost urgency and, thereafter, ensure effective implementation of the same. Governments must give due respect to the trade union movement so that rights to collective bargaining and freedom of association are not jeopardised. One must not forget that if the adults are not enjoying their fundamental rights at work or are unemployed, they in all likelihoods would send their children to work. Corporates would have to work out innovative and efficient solutions to ensure that there are no child/human/labour rights violations in their supply chains. Civil society must efficiently extend all support to governments and corporates in the collective endeavour to uphold the best interest of all children.

Equity and egalitarianism is the fulcrum of a just, peaceful and humane society. Every global citizen must be given a due and fair share as enshrined in the Universal Declaration of Human Rights. It is the responsibility of each and every stakeholder to work towards infusing equity in the society.

Last but not least, 'ethic' is the fluid that polishes and sharpens all the five weapons that I have mentioned earlier. One cannot run away or hide from one's soul. Transparent, accountable and responsible behaviour by governments, corporates, civil society and global citizens can make this world a much better and safer place for children. It is completely up to us as to how we use these six weapons for their betterment. I am absolutely sure that if used prudently and with a heart that brims with love for them, a child-friendly world is definitely within our reach. Let's make it a reality.

❑

20
Child Labour — A Social Aberration

Despite several constitutional provisions and laws that safeguard the rights of children, India has the dubious distinction of having the largest number of child labourers in the world.* If one were to believe the government estimates, there are about 1.20 crore economically active children below the age of 14. Non-governmental sources estimate a staggering six crore children engaged as labourers. Almost 70 per cent of these children work in the agricultural sector, whereas the rest continue to languish in informal/unorganised sectors, like garment, embroidery, carpet weaving, glass bangles, brassware, shellac jewellery, sporting goods, leather/plastic goods, stone quarries, mica and coal mining, tea plantation, brick kilns, construction sites, roadside restaurants and domestic work.

India is the breeding ground for worst forms of child labour. At least one crore or one out of every six child labourers is trapped in slavery as bonded labourer. Tens of thousands of children are trafficked from one state to another on tall claims and false hopes of a decent life. Several others are trafficked across the national borders. India is known to be a destination for large number of Nepalese and Bangladeshi children. Child prostitution,

---

* In this impassioned write-up, the author holds a mirror to Indian society and highlights how hypocrisy and apathy have resulted in persistence of child labour across the country despite laws.

child marriages, *devadasis*, forced amputation and beggary, children misused/abused by militant groups are some of the many forms of contemporary slavery that widely persist.

The push factors behind this social evil include abject poverty, illiteracy, lack of awareness, gullibility of parents, child-unfriendly mindset of the communities, socio-cultural discrimination, gender bias, poor outreach of legal safeguarding and ensuing development, absence of/or poor education facilities, state's incapability to effectively handle natural disasters, like flood, earthquakes, droughts and famines, hazards, like deforestation, mining and displacement are largely responsible for children falling prey to child labour. On the other hand, the insatiable greed on the part of employers who always scout for vulnerable, docile and cheap workforce, prevalence of corruption and apathy among the law enforcement agencies coupled up with connivance between traffickers and employers are some of the key factors that pull children towards labour.

Children are preferred over adults because they are unable to unionise, they do not demand decent work and never do they resort to strikes. We should remember that each child is employed at the cost of an adult's job. India has six crore child labourers and about 6.5 crore unemployed adults. Several studies have revealed that most of the jobless adults are parents of full-time child labourers. This is a vicious circle. No country could ever possibly solve the problem of poverty, unemployment and illiteracy without eliminating child labour.

Globalisation, privatisation and liberalisation have fuelled a massive demand for cheap and docile labour in production supply chains. Similarly, the ever-expanding middle class is always on a lookout for children to employ them as domestic help, for looking after their toddlers besides performing the usual household chores without a whimper.

A common notion that ubiquitously prevails is that poverty is the root cause of child labour, but it is a half-baked truth because the fact of the matter is that child labour creates and perpetuates intergenerational poverty. Child labourers are cursed to reel under poverty for the rest of their lives. In most cases, inhuman working conditions severely affect children's tender organs, thereby drifting them towards occupational diseases. Children engaged in agriculture are exposed to pesticides, insecticides and heavy machinery. Such children gradually acquire incurable ailments and often meet with accidents that render them physically crippled. Many children handling toxic chemicals in factories and workshops are susceptible to similar risks. Children producing fire crackers to amuse and entertain others more often than not meet with devastating accidents. Sivakasi, Virud Nagar and Sattur are infamous for such accidents. Similarly, children working in stone quarries and mines are diagnosed with tuberculosis and silicosis. Thousands of children are compelled to work under inhuman conditions in glass bangle factories of Firozabad and brass workshops in Moradabad, Aligarh and Delhi only to burn their lungs and little fingers.

I have personally come across thousands of cases where children weaving carpets in Mirzapur-Bhadoi belt were diagnosed with incorrigible lung disease that cut their lives short, unfulfilling their penchant to sit on the plush carpets that they produced. Children stitching footballs and other sports goods seldom get an opportunity to play with them. Those slogging endlessly in garment sweatshops never get to see their mothers and sisters adorning the beautifully and intricately embellished ensembles produced by them. What a shame!!!

Prevalence of child labour is nothing short of utter disrespect not only towards the Constitution but also towards all the international declarations, treaties and conventions that have been promulgated in the past. Child labour and slavery are worst variants of human rights' violation. It is a crime and a social stigma. Child labour is the biggest obstacle in the way of education and development. It is a slap across the face of civilisations, cultures and religions. Child labour is an evidence of serious lack of political will and social concern. It denies freedom, dignity and fulfilled childhood simultaneously endangering the child's present and future.

India has several legislative provisions aimed towards children. There is a specific law, Child Labour (Prohibition and Regulation) Act, 1986, which is highly objectionable and incomplete. It does not prohibit all forms of child labour, thereby posing a serious contradiction to the recently passed Right to Free and Compulsory Education Act, 2010, which calls for compulsory schooling for all children up to the age of 14 years. How can one law be in contravention to the other law that allows children to remain at workplaces instead of classrooms?

Juvenile Justice (Care & Protection of Children) Act, 2000 is yet another law aimed at safeguarding the interests of children by guaranteeing freedom and childhood up to the age of 18 years, which again locks horns with Child Labour (Prohibition and Regulation) Act, 1986 that defines child as a person who has not completed 14 years. Similarly, the Bonded Labour System (Abolition) Act, 1976 prohibits any person from being employed as bonded labour. There are a plethora of other acts, like the Factories Act, 1948, Shop and Establishment Acts, the Minimum Wages Act, 1948, the Contract Labour (Regulation and Abolition) Act, 1970, the Mines Act, 1952, and so on that make references about child labour. Additionally, several landmark judgements have been pronounced by the Honb'le Supreme Court and state high courts bearing implications for the issue of child labour.

Ironically, there is a gross violation of all these provisions across the length and breadth of the country. Enforcement continues to be the biggest challenge, which directly stems from political/administrative will and competence/capacity of the Labour Inspectorate System.

Inadequate resources and the issue of non-assignment of responsibility and accountability further wreak havoc on account of feeble enforcement of laws.

There are many success stories and vicarious experiences towards eliminating child labour that are worth applauding. It is heartening to see that the civil society is highly proactive in challenging the statutory authorities and businesses, thereby holding them accountable for their actions or inactions. The government, as a result of mounting pressure exerted by the public on various occasions, has been compelled to amend the existing laws, enacting new legislation and launching new welfare schemes specifically aimed towards the well-being of children. Consumer campaigns have brought the mighty multinationals on their knees for implementing effective CSR strategies. The carpet industry is a good case in point, where successful interventions could bring down the number of child labourers from over 300,000 to as low as 60,000. Initiatives, like school enrolment campaigns have created a new demand for education among the poor even in the remotest areas. Raid and rescue operations by 'Bachpan Bachao Andolan' have generated unprecedented mass awareness and media interest besides judicial intervention and unrelenting pressure on the government.

India has tremendous potential and possibilities to eradicate child labour only if a concerted and integrated approach is adopted. As mentioned above, there exists a vibrant and agile civil society and there are significantly effective and important welfare schemes, like MNREGA, Sarva Shiksha Abhiyaan, Mid-Day Meal provision, etc. that are aimed at the well-being of children and the greater good of communities. It is, therefore, the dire need of the hour to build and institute a strong, cooperative and integrated approach that can take on the issue of child labour with an utmost sense of urgency. ❑

21
Child Labour in India — Challenges and Solutions

A question I was often asked after the Nobel Prize win in October 2014 is, "What has the Nobel changed for you?" My answer always is, "The issues I have been raising have finally been acknowledged by the international community at the highest level. Child labour is finally being considered a serious global problem by the society."*

India has the dubious distinction of being a country with the highest number of child labourers in the world. According to the NSSO (National Sample Survey Office), there are 49.8 lakh child labourers between the ages of five and 14 in India as per the latest data of 2009-10. The Census 2011 places the number at 43.5 lakhs. However, civil society sources claim the number to be much higher at more than five crores.

On my first day of school, I saw a cobbler boy of my age, mending shoes outside the school gate. I asked my teachers and family, "Why is the boy not in school like everyone else?" "He is poor. He is born to work," they said. That made me confused and angry. Even after more than 50 years, child labour is not treated as a serious problem in India. Just take a look around. Everywhere around

* In this write-up, the author points out how the state, civil society, media and other stakeholders can contribute in their own way to work towards eliminating child labour from the country.

us we see instances of children living off the streets, in restaurants, in illegal factories, on agriculture land and as domestic labour.

These sights are justified with the explanation, 'India is a poor country. Poor have to work.' Let me debunk this myth here. Child labour is an evil that perpetuates poverty. Poverty and child labour share a chicken-and-egg relationship. Child labour fosters a vicious circle of poverty and illiteracy because such children remain uneducated and perform unskilled repetitive tasks that erode their future employability. If poor children continue to be forced into labour instead of attending schools and gaining education, they'll grow up into weak and hapless individuals who are stuck in a never-ending cycle of poverty, illiteracy and abuse.

Therefore, it is imperative that poverty, illiteracy and child labour are targeted simultaneously. Poverty cannot be eliminated till child labour is eradicated. Similarly, it is not possible to end child labour completely without addressing parental poverty.

Often overlooked is the fact that children are doing the very jobs that regular adults would do. A child labourer works for 12 to 14 hours a day, which is double the hours of a verified adult worker and for lesser or no wage. This means that for each child labourer, two adult labourers are rendered unemployed. If each child would be placed in school and replaced with an adult labourer, unemployment and, hence, poverty would reduce.

It was almost four decades back in 1973 that the ILO (International Labour Organisation) passed the ILO Convention 138 on Minimum Age of Employment that prohibits any child under the age of 14 to be employed. A few years later, in 1999, with the passage of Convention 182 on Worst Forms of Child Labour, child slavery, child trafficking and involvement of children in hazardous work were banned. India has still not ratified these two fundamental conventions. India is one of only seven countries in the world, like Somalia, Tuvalu, Eritrea, etc. that have not ratified Convention 182.

A key reason of perpetration of child labour in India is lack of political will. Since 1950, the Indian Constitution prohibits any hazardous labour that poses health or psychological risks to children. But it took governments 26 years to frame a law against child labour. The CLPR (Child Labour Prohibition & Regulation) Act 1986 thus formulated, only prohibited employment of children under the age of 14 in hazardous conditions, which left almost 90 per cent of child labour out of its purview.

Even this weak law was not imposed effectively and between 1986 and 2012, only 49,019 cases were registered and only 4,774 defaulters were fined. Isn't it a clear case of failure of law that not even one offender has been sent to prison for the maximum term of two years under the CLPR Act?

It took governments another three decades to amend this law by coming out with the Child Labour (Prohibition & Regulation) Amendment Bill, 2012 that addresses the concerns of CLPR. This Bill makes any form of labour under 14 becoming illegal (apart from family enterprise), prohibits hazardous work for children between 15 and 18 and provides for higher punishments, but it has still not been brought into effect. Here's hoping that the government makes the passage of this Bill a priority.

A second key challenge is that government agencies have not been made answerable for their lack of efforts in reducing child labour. The carpet industry of Mirzapur, coal and mica mining industry of Jharkhand, lock factories in Aligarh, brass industry in Moradabad, firecracker factories in Sivakasi and *zari* embroidery shops in Delhi and Jalandhar, have long held lakhs of child labourers. Most of these have child welfare committees and SCPCR (State Commissions for Protection of Child Rights). These organisations have lakhs of budgetary allocations, but in three decades, there hasn't been a single instance where the head of a commission or committee has been asked to quit because of failure to control child labour in his or her area.

Another key challenge is the refusal of the government to acknowledge the extent of the problem of child labour in the country. There is a sea charge in the numbers given by the Census (around 45 lakhs) and the numbers by civil society (around five crores).

Even when the laws, budgets, schemes are formulated and implemented, there remains a need for teamwork between various departments. Ending child labour has to be a joint effort of the labour department, child welfare committees, women and child development committees, police, district magistrates, etc. in compliance with the Right to Education Act, 2009 and Juvenile Justice (Care and Protection of Children) Act, 2000.

The only sustainable method to achieving growth and alleviating poverty is prioritising education, which is the key to other human rights. If quality and equitable education that encourages entrepreneurship, ethics and equality is imparted, most social and economic issues can be solved.

For instance, almost all children attend school in Kerala. This remarkable achievement is the fruit of strong political will, social awareness, and impetus for free and quality education by the government. Similarly, child labour is comparatively lower where schemes like MNREGA (Mahatma Gandhi National Rural Employment Guarantee Act), Sarva Shiksha Abhiyaan, mid-day meals and those related to rural development are being efficiently implemented.

According to a study by BBA that evaluated 100 children in two different districts and who were rehabilitated after rescue. Eighty per cent of the children who were enrolled in a regular school programme were not re-trafficked.

Taking good practices from schemes that have worked internationally could be a good way in tackling child labour. A few years ago, the Government of Brazil had introduced a welfare scheme called 'Bolsa Familia' in which positive incentives were shared to send and keep their children in school.

Though the challenges are huge, solutions still exist. Three kinds of interventions are needed to counter child labour at the most inherent level. They are social, state and business interventions.

Social interventions mean that each one of us breaks out of the culture of silence. Let us pledge we'll not look away when we see injustice against a child but instead, report it to the authority. Let us pledge we'll demand our local MPs and MLAs to declare their stand on child rights during election campaigning. Let us pledge that we'll be conscious consumers, always discouraging services like child domestic help and use of products created through dubious ways. The youth have to realise that they're not the leaders of tomorrow, but of today. It is through their energy, idealism and knowledge that we can positively change the social fabric of India.

State intervention requires that laws against child labour be strengthened, aligned with international conventions and their enforcement made tighter. The government must give priority to rehabilitation schemes for rescued child labourers along with sufficient budgetary allocations. Increased political will compounded with proactive initiatives and regular monitoring mechanisms against any form of child violence are needed. Adequate budgetary allocation and investment in education, health and protection of children must be prioritised.

Business intervention is needed because no corporate business can flourish for long at the cost of child labour. Businesses have to realise that ample production and profits happen only when there is a skilled workforce. Forced, unfed and malnutritioned children are not a skilled workforce, while healthy, adult, skilled workers are. Industries and businesses cannot ignore national and international legislations and standards.

Media's vigilance and consumer awareness have exposed various businesses in the textile, shoes, sporting goods sector because of which these businesses have suffered severe social backlash and financial losses. The corporates must carry out due diligence to ensure no child labour is employed in any part of the supply chain and monitoring mechanisms are tightened.

Child labour has decreased in sectors, such as coco-farms, sporting goods, carpet-making, while that in agriculture, garment-industry and domestic households remain high. This is primarily because of the above-mentioned interventions at various stages.

I believe that if these measures are applied immediately and effectively, it is possible to completely eliminate child labour in India and that too within our lifetime.

❑

22

Time to Save Childhood

India's children have been observing 14th November as their day for so many years. But this year is a bit different as they would celebrate it with a gift of Nobel Peace Prize. This is recognition of children's voices and faces which remain subdued and invisible for ages. Therefore, I have dedicated this Nobel Peace Prize to the world's children. I always feel myself one among them. For me, childhood has never been an age factor. It's a value to be preserved for the whole life. With such virtues, life becomes simpler and the world much more beautiful and safer.

Today, we are confronted with many serious problems, crises and scandals but the denial of childhood is the biggest scandal of our times. I strongly feel that the world has the potential to achieve the four Rs that I believe in. The first being Remembering our own childhood, then Recognising the issue of modern-day slavery and child exploitation, Respecting their journey from utter despair to unprecedented hope and, finally, Restoring their childhood through raising consciousness. We must not forget that all of us have our own children, grandchildren, sisters, brothers and children of friends too.*

In fact, each one of us has had the privilege of being a child once in our lifetime. Remembering this would mean

---

* In this column, the author argues how child labour and slavery can be abolished from the world in one generation if all stakeholders work together.

acknowledging the need for protection, love, joy, freedom and education which every child has the right to attain. It would also help us understand the beauty of simplicity and innocence which is immensely deteriorating in the personal and societal lives of people. Redeeming these elements of childhood is not only an act of humanity but a prerequisite to create a safer world. Many people today are unaware or believe that slavery of children is a thing of medieval age. It is quite prevalent and continuing shamelessly. In fact, as you read this, 17 crore children are languishing as child labourers in the entire world, out of which 8.5 crore enslaved, trafficked and used as child soldiers, prostitutes, petty criminals or child beggars as well as are exposed to the most dangerous and hazardous work that one can think of. This fact has to be recognised by everyone as a vital challenge. We are proud of our times witnessing or being part of a new civilisation of information and communication that has digitalised everything, including human sentiments and sensitivity. But, at the same time, every day 22,000 children die due to poverty. So, the big question is, 'Whose fault is it? Who is to be blamed?' One must understand that these enslaved children are not the subject of pity and every child is born with divine universal, constitutional and legal rights. Right to freedom and learning is the most important fundamental right and it shouldn't be compromised under any condition. I do not believe in work as charity. What I aspire and try to do is to ensure the right of children that were robbed off by vested interests. Freedom is divine and slavery is a design and supposition of man. Therefore, it can never remain immortal. Freedom will prevail eventually. Hence, we together must develop a child-friendly universe where respect and friendliness with children becomes the way of life. I firmly believe that childhood must be restored as the top priority in our personal, political and social life. Every child must be free from exploitative labour as it denies education and future opportunities, creating a vicious circle with adult unemployment and poverty. Look at the painful paradox, while 17 crore children are in full-time jobs, approximately 20 crore adults remain jobless. These adults are no one else but the very parents of the child labourers.

One has to break this cycle by ending child labour. This is not impossible. As I always say that India may be a country of hundred problems but it also is motherland of thousand solutions. Collective actions, political will, adequate resources and empathy for deprived children can and will end child labour. As child labour entails violence, denial of education is also violence against children. India has the greatest tradition of solving its major problems in the most non-violent and peaceful manner. We should work towards a child-friendly environment and realise the indomitable power of youth. On this important event, I give you all a slogan, "Globalise empathy, democratise knowledge and universalise rights."

23

Gifts of God Strewn on Streets

India is a land of great civilisations, cultures, religions and heritage. No other country in this world could boast of secular coexistence of the magnitude that exists in India. Places of worship were built, nurtured, respected and guarded jointly by the people of different religions. However, communal politics has shamed the rich heritage at several places on many occasions. Ayodhya is one of them.*

I had an opportunity to visit Ayodhya for the first time earlier last week, on an invitation from a spiritual institution, "Ramayanam Trust" headed by Sadhvi Mandakini Ramkinkar, who is truly engaged in teaching ideal and human values. I am quite aware of the ongoing controversy over Ramjanmabhoomi (the birthplace of Lord Rama) and the entire imbroglio surrounding it. Avadh is the land which sparked the first revolt for freedom against the British. It is also the land of peace-loving citizens who maintained their calm while many towns and cities were burning under the ire of communal violence soon after the demolition of the Babri Masjid structure in 1992.

What concerns me now is a stark contrast that is not uncommon in such holy cities. Out of sheer curiosity

---

* This column was written after the author visited Ayodhya, celebrated as the birthplace of Lord Rama. He was shocked and saddened to see the widespread use of child labour there, just as in other places in India.

and inquisition, a few friends and I along with my wife Sumedha, went to visit the disputed land. It was an awfully inconvenient experience because we were made to cross nearly six security posts where we were physically frisked and were scanned by metal detectors each time. With thousands of local policemen and personnel from the paramilitary forces deputed at every nook and corner, the city was appearing nothing short of a fortress. It was really scary to walk through a long maze that looked like an iron cage. Such stringent security circuit may not have existed even during the reigns of King Dashratha and Lord Rama to guard the real empire at its pink.

When we came out of the disputed site, we were completely exhausted and thirsty. To my surprise, pain and anguish, it was hard to find even a single restaurant in the vicinity and Hanuman Garhi area devoid of child labour. Somehow we managed to find one restaurant where thankfully no child was seen working. While we were having water and buttermilk at that restaurant to quench our thirst, several child beggars who were shabbily clad and bare foot inadvertently surrounded our car.

What a glaring paradox it is! Crores of rupees are being spent to guard a disputed piece of land which has a devastated structure and loads of debris piled upon. It is true that this land has been a pie of faith for millions of fanatics who are sentimentally bonded with it, but where do these children figure in our religious schemes? Ironically, similar sentiments cannot be seen towards those children who are being robbed of their childhood every single minute that passes.

This is not any different from the vicinity of Ajmer Sharif, Golden Temple, Se Cathedral, Goa, Deoband and Jama Masjid areas where large number of children can be seen toiling at all times. Child beggars are most common. Millions of devotees throng these pilgrim spots every year. Billions of rupees are collected as offerings. It is time we honestly asked ourselves, "Are these children not off-springs of God?", "Are they not the most precious gifts of Almighty?", "What do religions, faith and holy books have to say about such children?" Nobody seems to be interested in answering these questions at all. People conveniently turn their blind eye and deaf ears towards the issue of child labour.

Almost at all pilgrim towns, children are coerced to work. Some of them are made to beg with their hands and limbs deliberately amputated to seek public sympathy. Child hawkers perpetually engaged by other people to sell commodities on their behalf cannot be termed as child entrepreneurs by any stretch of imagination. They are child labourers. Some children in these holy towns are engaged in professions as ghastly as prostitution.

In religious institutions and seminaries, child rights are outrageously violated. There exists widespread economic and sexual exploitation behind the closed doors. Time and again, these shocking revelations have been unearthed in church dormitories and in accommodations where *devadasis* reside. It is pitiable that clerics and holy men are equal accomplices in rearing child labour. Not too long ago there were news stories all over the media unearthing a nexus between clerics, child-traffickers and slave masters. Children from places like Saharsa, Madhubani, etc. are trafficked under false hopes of getting shelter in *madarsas* (seminaries) in Delhi. Many a time, clerics of source and destination areas shake hands to execute mass child-trafficking plans which promote unabated child labour.

I have survived several formidable attacks endangering my life, when *maulavis* (clerics) and communal leaders in a bid to hide their own follies instigated the mob against my team during raid-and-rescue operations. They took advantage of emotionally charged communities and made them to attack the activists of 'Bachpan Bachao Andolan' by spreading rumours that we were trying to snatch children away from the *madarsa* (seminary). One such attack took place in Delhi in the month of March earlier this year where four activists were brutally injured. The matter was subsequently taken up by the Delhi High Court, whereby directives were issued to the law enforcement and administrative agencies to provide adequate protection to child rights activists during raid-and-rescue operations.

Undoubtedly, the outreach and impact of preaching of clerics and holy men who appear round the clock on national television channels is far more than that of any state-sponsored advertisement or NGO campaign for that matter. Unfortunately, mass media is often misused or bought by such holy men for fulfilling their selfish motives, like image makeover, reaping commercial benefits, as well as promotion of their sects and spreading superstitions, orthodoxy in the society. Had these people been slightly sensitive towards the plight of millions of Indian children and honestly adhered to the preaching underpinned in the holy books and epics, the situation could have been a lot brighter and better than what it is today. Six crore children would not have been reeling under endemic child labour. Instead, they could have been attaining quality and meaningful education at school like other privileged children. Social aberrations and gender bias, like female infanticide, would not have taken a toll on the sex ratio which at present stands at 918 females for every 1,000 males, 70 per cent male children would not have fallen prey to pedophiles, 53 per cent female children would not have been sexually violated. This country could have been so very child-friendly.

❑

24

Obstacles in the Attainment of Primary Education

The report card of the country on right to education even after completing more than a year is not very encouraging. Although there has been a significant increase in budgetary allocation, there exist serious challenges to access, inclusion and quality of education. India, one of the most promising economies and the largest democracy in the world, still has the stigma of having the largest number of illiterate women and men and out-of-school children. Every third illiterate person in this world is an Indian.*

Education for all children between the ages of six and 14 is a legal right since last April, but the whole year has not brought much good news. The Union Minister himself agrees that enrolment rates in primary classes have decreased and independent researches reveal that the quality and equity of education have also fallen.

Education has been enshrined as a fundamental human right by the United Nations since 1949 but India amended its Constitution in this respect only in 2001. This was possible due to a strong and persistent civil society movement. It is also important to know that it took nine years to translate this constitutional provision into enforceable legislation, i.e. the Right to Education Act. But, according to a recent

---

* This column was written one year after India passed a law making education a fundamental right of every child. It analyses how universal primary education remains a dream that faces many hurdles.

study, only 6 per cent people in the country are aware that education now is a legal right.

This lethargic attitude speaks volumes towards strengthening the argument for the utter lack of political will in this country. This clearly reflects the failure in identifying and addressing the most fundamental challenges in attaining education for our children. Considering the decrease in primary school enrolment rates, one must try to find an answer to three simple questions. Who are these out-of-school children?, Where are they?, and, why are they not in classrooms?

The first issue regarding these is the confusion on existing data. The government claims that 75 lakh children are out of school (based on the 2001 Census report). If we take in account the latest NSSO report, the figure goes up to 2.1 crores. On the other hand, the demographic projection shows that India must have 22 crore children in 2011, out of which 16 crore attend school. This would mean that six crore are out of school. This figure corroborates with the non-governmental estimates of five crore children engaged in various forms of child labour. The situation requires utmost clarity on the statistics because this has direct implications on state policies and budgetary allocations when dealing with these issues.

The out-of-school children, whatever be their number, are not sitting idle at home. They are hardest to reach or are the children of socially, economically or politically excluded families or are victims of age-old discriminatory cultural practices and gender bias. Crores of them are engaged as child labourers. Many are bonded and trafficked. A large number are trapped in factories, mines and agriculture fields or forced to live in domestic servitude, and so, how can they possibly be present in classrooms?

So far, no sincere effort has been made by the government to address this serious obstacle. This requires a thorough identification and social and geographical mapping exercises, additional resources, innovative techniques including preventive measures, engagement of communities including cultural and religious groups, etc. Moreover, this also calls for expansion of endeavours beyond the education sector. An effective policy coherence and genuine coordination among various ministries, like Labour, Women and Child Welfare, Social Justice, Rural Development, Home Affairs, Health and Education is imperative because the Ministry of Education alone cannot ensure the freedom, withdrawal, repatriation, rehabilitation, health and safety of the hard-to-reach children.

Also, in the present context of a global economic recession, food crises, and environmental challenges, a broad multi-stakeholder partnership is essential, particularly, a genuine public-private partnership, with a caution that it should not lead to the privatisation and commercialisation of a fundamental right is important.

The second major obstacle in the enrolment and retention of children in schools is the overall poor quality of the public education system. Firstly, in spite of clear recommendations from all state-sponsored commissions on education during the last several decades to invest at least 6 per cent of the total GNP for education, the government is still nowhere near this target. Neither the federal nor the provincial governments have ever considered education for poor children a political priority. Secondly, the RTE law is silent on the common school system. The state policies have reduced the fundamental right of education to a mere commodity. The rich can buy the best that is available and the poor are denied even the bare minimum. Thirdly, it is the children that remain the worst sufferers of poor and corrupt education governance.

It would be pertinent to mention the facts revealed in three most recent researches and public hearings conducted by Pratham (ASER, 2010), BBA (Public Hearing on Education, 2011) and National Coalition for Education (Edwatch Report, 2011). According to the ASER Report, almost half of all 5th grade children in government schools lack the reading skills expected at second grade. The same report also underlines a decline in overall Maths skill in children between 2009 and 2010. Only 65 per cent first grade children can recognise the numbers one to nine in comparison to almost 70 per cent a year ago. The ASER Report also states a decrease in popularity of government schools over private ones in rural areas, which has resulted in a significant growth in enrolment in private schools from 21.8 per cent in 2009 to 24.3 per cent in 2010.

The third hindrance to the provision of basic education is the lack of basic amenities and requirements in schools. The public hearings conducted by BBA in nine states in India reveal that only 60 per cent primary school-going children have access to clean drinking water. There are no functional toilets for more than 50 per cent students and in case of girls, the situation is even worse as only 30 per cent have access to toilet facilities. This directly impacts the dropout rates substantially, especially among girls. Also, it was seen that only one-third of all schools have a playground and only 10 per cent children are provided with sports equipment and play material. Corruption with regards to the provision of mid-day meal was also seen everywhere, with both the quality and quantity of meals provided. The situation is compounded with paucity of an adequate number of teachers hired, high teacher absenteeism and significant school distances.

According to the Edwatch Report, more than half of all existing upper primary schools are at distances ranging from three to 10 kilometres.

The above-mentioned obstacles to education for our children are not incorrigible. If we have a deep sense of urgency, adequate political will, appropriate budgetary spending, as well as a comprehensive and time-bound action plan with concrete intra-agency coordination and a clear accountability framework, India can not only enforce the present law, but will be able to attain all internationally pledged education for all goals.

❑

25

Giving Childhood a Miss yet Again?

Once again the nation is on the verge of failing millions of its children who are victims of a composite and organised crime of trafficking, sexual exploitation including rape and forced labour. The provisions of trafficking and employment of a trafficked person including defining, criminalising and penalising various aspects of such crimes that were included in the ordinance promulgated in February are not being included in the draft of Criminal Law (Amendment) Bill, 2013.* This is a sad reflection on our political class in addressing complex social crimes in entirety and with a sense of urgency. The law-makers have conveniently or conspicuously chosen to remain silent and non-committal on this extremely imperative issue.

Even after 63 years of our Constitution being in force, Article 23 that prohibits traffic in human beings, *begar* and other similar forms of forced labour and deems it an offence punishable in accordance with law is being outrightly violated. India has ratified Palermo Protocol on trafficking in persons in 2011, which makes it binding for the republic to calibrate its national legislation according to the provisions of the international convention. The Supreme Court of India has already accepted the definition of human trafficking. The

* Written in 2013, the author argues in the column how the government and law-makers are failing the children of India by enacting inherently weak laws. Years of sustained efforts have now led to the process of enacting more effective anti-trafficking laws in 2017.

promulgation of Criminal Law (Amendment) Ordinance, 2013 paved the ground for a reasonably robust legislation linking the issue of missing children with their trafficking and exploitation for forced labour for the first time ever.

Sections 370 and 370A of the ordinance had made trafficking in all its forms and manifestations including abduction, harbouring, sexual exploitation, forced labour, etc., a cognisable offence with stringent penalties. These sections not only addressed the crime of sexual exploitation but also criminalised the processes that lead to sexual exploitation and several other forms of abuses.

It is a sorry state of affairs that 11 children reportedly go missing every hour in our country with only one criminal case of investigation being registered while almost half of them remain untraced. Earlier last month, the Supreme Court bench headed by none other than the Chief Justice of India, acknowledging the gravity of the pressing situation of missing children, rapped the Union and state governments and went to the extent of exclaiming, "Nobody seems to be concerned about the missing children; they (governments) are playing the fool with the court." 'Bachpan Bachao Andolan', the petitioner in this matter, has been repeatedly arguing that these children essentially are victims of organised crime of human trafficking and are sold for flesh trade, forced beggary, bonded labour and organ sale.

Usha (name changed), now fifteen had been kidnapped from her village in Lakhimpur district of Assam when she was barely five years old. She remained untraced for nine years. She was sold from one employer to another as a domestic worker in Delhi before being finally rescued by 'Bachpan Bachao Andolan' in November 2012 from the clutches of a placement agency that was exploiting her in every single manner possible. Let's face it. Usha did not disappear in thin air. She was a victim of trafficking that is fast emerging as the most lucrative crime in the world, along with drugs and arms.

Usha was brought to Delhi by somebody and exchanged hands as though she were a commodity. Upon being rescued, all that the girl complained for was non-payment of her wages. She remained tight-lipped about the physical, sexual and mental exploitation that she had been through. Probably, wages was the maximum that she perceived as justice. Such vulnerable children are seldom aware of their rights. Since Usha was not formally engaged for commercial sexual exploitation, the provisions of Immoral Traffic (Prevention) Act could not be invoked. She was above 14 when rescued; therefore, child labour law was not applicable in her case. In the absence of any clearly defined legal statutes in our country, Usha could not be categorised as a missing child, child labourer or a victim of trafficking for that matter.

It is disquieting to note that trafficking for sexual exploitation is fast becoming a coordinated and organised crime under the garb of massage parlours, bar dancing and 'placement agencies' that traffic girls across the country in the name of domestic or other labour, and exploit them both economically and sexually. There is no legal protection for these girls as victims of trafficking in the new draft that is being proposed by the government.

In a recent incident, 284 children were rescued and 55 child-traffickers were arrested from various West Bengal-bound trains in Bharatpur and Jaipur. These children were being transported to Bihar and West Bengal. Clearly, they were in transit and were not rescued from the workplace, so they did not fall under the purview of child labour law. This could have actually made way for an easy escape for the culprits. However, these traffickers could be appropriately booked on the spot under Sections 370 and 370A, which are thankfully still in force until the ordinance is replaced by the proposed law that is to be tabled in the Parliament next week. Thus, it is more than evident that the importance of the comprehensive definition of trafficking in persons and the employment of trafficked persons cannot be emphasised enough. If these sections are excluded from the legislation, it would be next to impossible to incriminate such people who ruin innocent childhoods for their vested interests.

Removal or dilution of the aforesaid sections from the proposed Criminal Law (Amendment) Bill, 2013 will be nothing short of a cruel joke on the women and children who only get justice once it is established that they have gone missing for the purpose of trafficking and sexual exploitation. Why head towards a legislation that is curative and narrow in nature when we have preventive and replicable provisions in the ordinance to emulate from?

❑

26

Peace or War! — Time to Think Seriously

It is exciting! It is encouraging! It is historical! It brings enormous hope for the future. And it is not just an ordinary demonstration, but a mass quest for peace. The past weeks have witnessed millions of people on the streets around the world, with protests and slogans to stop the war. There were grandparents holding the fingers of their grandchildren in one hand and a peace placard in another, the parents of September 11 victims and the children of martyrs of the Second World War to turn to peace activists, expressing their serious concerns against war.

In India, hundreds of former child labourers and school-going children along with teachers, parents, social workers, artists and politicians had a day-long peace prayer at Rajghat, Mahatma Gandhi's memorial in New Delhi. Challenging questions were raised by some youngsters like Om Prakash, Shahzad and Sunita, as to why children always become the worst sufferers of war and why the politicians and adults cannot give a second thought to their plight before opting for it. One of them also said, "If you kill our fathers before our eyes, do you think we will ever sit at rest? You will give birth to numerous terrorists if you drop bombs on our families." Another asked, "If you cannot give us peace and childhood, what right do you have to rob them from us?"

This mass upsurge for peace has proved those wrong who were under the impression that there is only one superpower left in the post-Cold War. In fact, another is born, that is, the people's power, which at least has delayed, if not fully stopped the United States and its alliance in their decision of war on Iraq.* Thousands of Iraqi children and their families' lives are about to vanish if the war is launched. Beyond the moment of the war, the nation will lose generations of innocent smile and hope, which cannot be easily restored after such trauma. Thousands of them will be abandoned on the streets and in unchained cycle of poverty, illiteracy, child labour and loss of hope.

Is it not a shame that the world is not prepared to spend an additional 10 billion dollars to protect all its children from exploitation and to ensure their education which amounts to nothing but four days of military expenditure? Is it not a greater shame that when most people want to live in peace, a few powerful politicians often manage to find excuses or raise age-old arguments that war is a necessity and an inevitable solution to buy peace? Sadly, we have produced enough weapons to destroy the entire humanity but not enough life-saving medicines, safe drinking water, books and toys for our children.

Even before a war is launched in Iraq, the economic embargo imposed on the country for over the last 10 years has led to a massive impoverishment of the country. Due to lack of basic facilities, especially food and medicine, more than 1.7 million Iraqis died — almost a third of the lives lost are of children who never had a chance to live their lives. Even if they had survived to live, 8,00,000 children suffered from malnutrition. WHO and UNICEF reports show that 6,000 children below the age of five years die each month

* This column was written after an alliance led by the United States launched a war against Iraq in the aftermath of the 9/11 terror attack. The author demands that world leaders must not make children victims of these conflicts.

in Iraq, affected by the ignorance of the impact of war on people. Why should these innocent people pay a heavy price due to Saddam or any other?

To highlight a few more alarming facts, the military expenditure over the past two years has increased in all the regions. The steepest rises were in Africa and Asia. Of the 25 conflicts in the year 2000, greatest numbers were in these two regions. The situation has been worse during the last decade. Asia, which has about 40 per cent of the world's child labour force spends about 115 billion dollars on military and has witnessed an increase of 50 per cent in military expenditure over the last decade. Similarly, the African region spends 14 billion dollars on military with 20 per cent increase in the same period with 30 per cent of child labour. Also Latin America with 50 per cent increase in military budget in the same period with 30 billion current spending on military has 20 per cent of child labour force.

According to a study, an estimated number of dead and wounded civilians will be at least 5,00,000 if just conventional weapons are used. Nobody is able to predict the damage if nuclear weapons are used. Only the knowledge of our history can answer how devastating it would be. The United States has not ruled out the possibility of using nuclear weapons, if the situation demands so. Wars in themselves are highly destructive, leading to a huge amount of displacement of people in the affected zones. And if at all it materialises, you and I might have to watch unfortunate scenes on our television screens showing that the fastest and the most sophisticated guided missiles are bombing Baghdad.

The dangerous reality is that the technological advancement has always been used as the most effective weapon for mass destruction and violence. There is no doubt that many of the weapons and strategies designated for 'the defence' are increasingly irrelevant to the real underlying instabilities and dangers facing their people. Armaments have always been the examples of misused technology, right from the invention of a sharp stone to kill animals to swords, spears, arrows, guns, cannons and nuclear, chemical and biological weapons. The resilience in the expenditure is a cause of concern to us all since so many human development challenges still need to be addressed in these regions — homes to largest concentrations of poor, illiterate and the exploited.

Of course, one must not ignore the dangers of terrorism. Many countries have been facing the curse for years, but it did not acquire so much momentum on the world agenda. Once again the most shameful incident of September 11 has exposed the ugly face of terror. We should recognise and respect the sentiments of the people of US and elsewhere, but revenge is no solution. Similarly, the alleged production and procurement of biological and chemical weapons of mass destruction by Baghdad or any other country is a matter of serious concern. They must be unearthed wherever they are and destroyed without a second thought, keeping in mind that war is not the only remedy. Any war, violence or destruction causes unprecedented hatred and revenge, which may result in extremism, terrorism and destruction.

I am writing this not with any ideological, geo-political or religious sentiments, but with a deep concern for the innocent children in Iraq, who may be punished for no fault of theirs. My friends, another war is in the offing, another death of peace efforts is on its way to glory, another seed for future revenge is sown and another blot is waiting to be put on the face of humankind. Such a war would have very serious long-term repercussions and definitely there would be worldwide reactions to it.

Today, on behalf of millions of children and peace-loving people, we must speak up and stand for peace, as peace is not just the privilege of George Bush or Tony Blair or any other politician. It is our birthright — the right of every human being. I propose that without getting into any political debate, we should raise our voice for peace, as well as against the very culture of war which eventually deprives millions of other children from their childhood, smile, protection and education.

❑

27

Taking on the Circus

About 30 years ago, when I decided to declare war against child servitude, it was like chasing a wild goose in the dark since child labour was not even considered an issue and was treated as a way of life. There was nothing substantive to learn from or seek support for, except trying to emotionally sensitising and rationally convincing the people around.

The corrupt polity and enforcement machinery, lack of political will, poor sensitivity, age-old mind-sets, scarcity of resources, absence of legal support and protection were among the biggest obstacles that came my way. It has been an equally big challenge to survive amidst danger, threats and formidable attacks, times innumerable when I have missed death by a whisker.

Recently, the Supreme Court has ruled that child labour in circuses be banned, compelling the government to make amendments in child labour law. You may be aware that not too long ago, me and my colleagues from the BBA (Bachpan Bachao Andolan) had taken on the circus industry, where a large number of children, particularly girls, were being treated worse than animals.* They have been trafficked, kidnapped and brought to work in circuses where physical

---

* In this moving account, the author remembers how he and his associates faced violence, apathy and worse when they struggled to stop the exploitation of children in circuses. He eventually won the war when the Supreme Court banned child labour in circuses.

torture and sexual abuse is a norm. These circuses are nothing short of fortresses. In the summer of 2004, I led a secret raid along with a team of parents, magistrates, police and colleagues from BBA to rescue about 12 girls held in bondage for years.

Soon after, we were allowed entry inside the residential tented area by the circus proprietor, the atmosphere turned violent. The proprietor along with his men started shouting at us, claiming that there weren't any girls. All of a sudden, the flabbergasted owner pulled out his pistol at me. As luck would have it, the video camera of a TV channel was on. With the camera exposed, the conniving police personnel on the spot advised the owner to hide his gun as the footage was being captured in the recording device.

The owner immediately pulled his pistol back but ordered his people to kill me and my colleagues. In this murderous attempt, six of us were gravely injured and had to be rushed to the hospital by passers-by. Since we failed to rescue the girls, I announced a fast-unto-death in protest against this social evil on the second day of my being discharged by the hospital.

We tried to build a strong public movement around this issue and simultaneously approached the High Court. Finally, complying with the order issued by the court, 24 girls were rescued. Subsequently, we moved the SC, seeking a permanent remedy and succeeded against all odds.

Yet another incident that I can recount occurred in 1989 when after rescuing 14 bonded child labourers from a carpet-weaving unit near Allahabad, I was waiting at the Mirzapur railway station for the train back to Delhi on a freezing winter night. I saw at least 30-40 scantily-clad children shivering on the other platform on the station. These children were in a group and were being chased and steered by a man as though they were cattle. When I intervened and questioned the trafficker, a policeman who was an accomplice in this act manhandled me and locked me up in a cell at the railway station itself. Throughout the night, I kept sitting on a stone bench inside the cell without a blanket. For a few hours, I was annoyed and upset at the whole incident, but gradually as the night passed, realisation dawned upon me that rescuing a few children here and there would make no dent. I realised that the demand for child labourers who come cheap and easy was on the same wavelength as the demand for Indian carpets in Western markets.

In the morning when I was freed from the lock-up, I walked out with a new lease of commitment and called up my German supporter, Rainer Kruse later in the evening to launch a carpet consumers' campaign. I was completely cognizant of the risk that the Indian carpet industry ran towards a total ban on the product in Western markets. I engineered a technique for individually accrediting child labour-free carpets, which eventually resulted in the first-ever social label of child labour-free goods in the world, popularly known as Rugmark. It was obviously difficult to proselytise European charities to join me in this campaign, at a time when the phenomenon of corporate social responsibility had not been discovered.

Initially, the industry and its allies in the government brandished me a traitor for ruining the economy. This did not deter me. Today, one-third of the total carpet traded from South Asia is Rugmark-certified and there exists no other example where the number of child and bonded labourers has decreased from ten lakhs to barely three lakhs, as it happened in South Asia.

❑

28

Who will Bring the Missing Children Back Home?

The most charming and ever-smiling Vishal will be missed by everyone at Bal Ashram. He indeed was very special among those 100 rescued child and bonded labourers who are presently undergoing rehabilitation at this centre in Virat Nagar, near Jaipur. Vishal never took more than a minute to make friends out of strangers. Whoever came in contact with Vishal, be it a local villager or an international guest, was completely charmed. Some distinguished people who always looked for Vishal include Marc Dullaert, Chairman, founder of Kids Rights Foundation and children's ombudsman at The Netherlands and the Swedish designer, businessman Stanley Bains. Both of them are ardent supporters of Bal Ashram. After twists and turns for nearly four years, Vishal is back home and has been finally reunited with his parents earlier last week. The day of this re-union was that of great jubilation, when emotions were at the peak.*

The mother who had lost all hopes of meeting her son ever again, hugged Vishal and the joy of that tearful reunion cannot be described in words. This was the moment of truth that moistened the eyes of everybody present over

* In this column written in 2011, the author passionately argues about creating institutional systems that could help trace missing children. The movement won a big victory when it was made mandatory for police stations to register cases of missing children.

there. Owing to the unrelenting efforts of the authorities at Bal Ashram and police, the boy's whereabouts could be successfully traced barely twenty-four hours before the repatriation. The police of Pilibanga block of Ganganagar in Rajasthan (i.e. the place where Vishal hailed from) had arranged for a telephonic call between the father and the son. Vishal could immediately recognise his father's voice at the other end. This bore a spark on Vishal's face. He hysterically ran across, hugging his friends, teachers and even pets in pure blithe giving goosebumps to all those who stood watching him.

Vishal's parents had spent a fortune in tracing their missing child all these years. They cooled their heels off, frenetically praying at temples and *mazars* in search of their son. They were absolutely zapped to see their son not only hale and hearty but doing well in studies. Vishal had not started going to school at the time when he had suddenly gone missing in 2007.

'Bachpan Bachao Andolan' rescued Vishal along with six other children who were enslaved and trapped by drug traffickers and criminals. He was subsequently brought to Bal Ashram and was given special care and protection. He was unable to recall his address and father's name, so it was all the more difficult to trace his parents. Bal Ashram's management could somehow trace Vishal's faint memories and dialect back to his village.

Unfortunately, all stories do not end on a happy note as the one you just went through. Nearly 66,000 children go missing every year in India. In fact, one child goes missing every eight minutes. In Delhi alone, on an average seven children went missing every day in June 2011. The daily average for the entire year stood at six.

The connotation missing children in itself is quite misleading. Children are not objects. Unlike inanimate things, such as mobile phones, pens, bicycles or umbrellas, children are living beings who cry and shout for food,

With the Nobel Peace Prize in Oslo, Norway (10 December, 2014)

Dedicating the Nobel medal to the nation by presenting it to President Shri Pranab Mukherjee (7 January, 2015)

Kailash Satyarthi with the President Shri Ram Nath Kovind at the conclusion of Bharat Yatra against child sexual abuse & trafficking (2017)

In discussion with Prime Minister Shri Narendra Modi for eradication of child labour in India (2015)

With the Vice President of India Shri M. Venkaiah Naidu (2017)

Calling for education to be made a fundamental right under the Constitution with the then Prime Minister Shri Atal Bihari Vajpayee (2000)

Meeting the then President Shri K.R. Narayanan to demand that education be made a fundamental right (2001)

At an event organised by Bachpan Bachao Andolan with the then Vice-President Shri Bhairon Singh Shekhawat (2003)

Urging the then Prime Minister Shri Inder Kumar Gujral to take measures to protect children from violence (1998)

Meeting Leader of Opposition Smt. Sonia Gandhi for the Child-friendly village programme (2015)

With Shri Amitabh Bachchan during the show,
'Kaun Banega Crorepati' after Bharat Yatra

With friend and industrialist Shri Rahul Bajaj
during the Bharat Yatra

With Hon'ble Chief Justice of India Justice Shri Dipak Misra (2016)
(Launching of the book 'Azad Bachpan Ki Ore')

With the Hon'ble Chief Justice of India Shri T.S. Thakur (2015)

With Prince Ali Bin Al Hussein, H.H. Dalai Lama, Shri Pranab Mukherjee, Princess Charlene of Monaco and Princess Laurentien of Netherlands during the 2016 Laureates & Leaders Summit for Children

Launching the Laureates & Leaders Summit, 2016 with a galaxy of Nobel Laureates and global leaders

With Madhya Pradesh Chief Minister Shri Shivraj Singh Chauhan and volunteers during Bharat Yatra (2017)

With Andhra Pradesh Chief Minister Shri N. Chandrababu Naidu leading a rally during Bharat Yatra

Kerala Chief Minister Shri Pinarayi Vijayan addressing a meeting during Bharat Yatra

Union Minister Shri Narendra Singh Tomar interacting with children (2014)

With former Union Labour Minister Shri Bandaru Dattreya (2016)

At a conference with the then Hon'ble Chief Justice of India Shri K.G. Balakrishnan (2008)

Seeking support for the inclusion of child slavery, child labour and trafficking in the Sustainable Development Goals from fellow Nobel Laureate and President of the United States of America Mr. Barack Obama, First Lady Michelle Obama, wife Sumedha Kailash and some children (2015)

With fellow Nobel Peace Laureate Mr. Muhammad Yunus (2015)

Walking with the then Prime Minister of the United Kingdom Mr. Gordon Brown to participate at an event for child labour in Delhi (2008)

At the launch of 'Speak Truth to Power' in Washington DC with the then President of the United States of America Mr. Bill Clinton, Ms. Kerry Kennedy and freed child slave Kalu Kumar (1999)

During the Global March against Child Labour with the then President of France Mr. Jacques Chirac (1998)

In deep conversation with American Senator Mr. Tom Harkin on issues of child slavery and human rights (1998)

Presenting a petition for the inclusion of child slavery, child labour and trafficking in Sustainable Development Goals signed by 5,50,000 people to the then United Nations Secretary General Mr. Ban Ki Moon (2015)

Culmination of Global March at United Nations Palace, Geneva, when Kailash Satyarthi along with some children was invited to address the International Labour Organisation convention in session (1998)

Attacked by circus mafia in a raid operation to rescue young Nepali girls who had been enslaved in Gonda district, Uttar Pradesh (2004)

In Pakistan during the Global March against Child Labour which traversed 80,000 kms across 103 countries (1998)

Global March against Child Labour in Costa Rica (1998)

Kailash Satyarthi leading the South Asian March against Child Trafficking in Bangladesh. The march travelled 15,000 kms and witnessed participation of a million people (2007)

South Asian March against Child Trafficking in Nepal (2007)

Leading a protest march with parents of missing children in New Delhi (2007)

During the Bharat Yatra against child labour (1994). Under Kailash Satyarthi's guidance, the march went across the nation covering 5,000 kms from Kanyakumari to New Delhi

Protest march against child labour in stone quarries of Faridabad region, Haryana (1981)

Leading a demonstration against child labour in Jaipur, Rajasthan (1982)

Promoting globalized compassion through the 100 Million for 100 Million Movement (2016)

Addressing the International Labour Organisation (June 2015)

Mr. Juan Manuel Santos, President of the Republic of Colombia and Kailash Satyarthi speaking during the Session 'Achieving Sustainable Peace in a Fractured World' at Davos (2018)

Leading the Bharat Yatra march with Sumedha Kailash

Kailash Satyarthi with children rescued from forced labour in a Delhi factory (2009)

Helping a child draw pencil portraits

With child workers of cocoa bean farms in Ivory Coast, West Africa (2012)

A selfie with his most beloved friends

A child's smile is the biggest inspiration for Kailash Satyarthi

water, shelter and place to sleep daily. Then why can't police and other state agencies trace them? The reason is fairly simple. There is no political will in the state agencies to trace children that are lured away, kidnapped, trafficked, detained and trapped by nefarious elements primarily to derive monetary benefits. Many of them are sold to work as bonded labourers or child prostitutes, as forced beggars, drug peddlers, etc. It has been unearthed that children are sold for trading illicit organs, legal adoption by infertile couples, as child brides to Middle East with men nearly five times their age or are even forced to become child combatants.

Most of the missing and untraced children come from economically weak families, migrants and slum dwellers that do not have the power and approach. So, they are conveniently ignored or mistreated by police. Sunita, whose eight-year-old son is missing since 2009 from west Delhi, told me, "Whenever I go to the police station to enquire about my son, they ask me to go and check on the Internet, I don't know what that is?" When Jameel, father of a 14-year-old missing girl went to lodge a complaint, the police officials went to the extent of saying that the girl might have eloped with her boyfriend. Is it not being completely insensitive?

One must not forget that trafficking of children and human beings is the third largest illicit trade in the world with an estimated annual worth of over ₹ 2 lakh crores. The biggest irony is that there is no clear definition of missing children in Indian law, which further causes confusion while registering the case at the police station in the first place.

Secondly, while the government admits that complaints for 1,17,000 missing children were received in the last two years, but it was only 16,000 FIRs that were eventually registered under the category of kidnapping. This is a very serious problem which requires immediate enactment/amendment in the law.

Thirdly, except for a direction by the Honb'le Delhi High Court, there are no standard operating procedures or guidelines for the law enforcement agencies.

Fourthly, there is no central agency for maintaining proper records of the children that are registered, traced or untraced for that matter.

Fifthly, there is no coordination between the existing agencies, like police, national, state, district crime record bureaus, civil society organisations, municipal or panchayat institutions and the anti-trafficking cells that were opened, of late in some states.

Sixthly, no systematic efforts have been made in sensitising and training the agencies dealing with cases of missing children as well as fixing accountability on them.

If the government is honest and serious enough to stop this menace and crime, such measures must be taken immediately.

❑

29

World Fit for Children

The world has never been unfit for the children of kings and queens and of those people who had control over power and wealth for ages. The world was always fit for children in the holy teachings. Jesus says let the children come to me first. The *Vedas* proclaimed that children are sacred souls and Islam taught to see the glow of God in the face of a child. I don't think that the world is too bad for the children of privileged elites in various societies.*

However, it is not fit for those millions of children of lesser gods who are sold and bought like animals, confined to the mines and brick kilns as slaves, locked in factories and houses, stitching soccer balls, polishing gems, carving wood, knotting carpets, working alongside the glass furnaces, trafficked for domestic labour, forced into beggary where sometimes their tiny organs are mutilated to gain more sympathy, or for those who are victims of armed conflicts, ethnic violence and even the victims of development-related displacement. It is also not fit for young girls trapped in the flesh trade, or for the kids who are tied down on the backs of camels in the Gulf countries where screaming of a child makes the camel run faster and his master happy. It is not fit for those who were denied

* In this piece written in 2002, when child rights and their right to freedom, education and dignity were still not debated widely, the author argues how humanity demands a society that is more compassionate towards children.

the basic right to education or forced to leave school due to poverty and unable to meet the fees and other expenses of schooling.

The world was not fit for Gulabo, who had her last breath in my lap. For 14-year-old girl Gulabo, education meant life and liberty.

Her father worked as a slave labourer at brick kilns for years together with his family. Gulabo was born and brought up as a slave and was afflicted with severe malnutrition and tuberculosis. They were tortured and abused, sexually, physically and mentally. They were never paid any wages except for poor quality food to barely survive. A few years back, with the help of the Supreme Court of India, I liberated this family and 27 others in a secret raid. When I brought them to my office, the condition of Gulabo deteriorated and she collapsed. Her last words were, "I want to live, mother." When her father, accompanied by me, was asked to sign the papers to release the dead body from the mortuary, he said, "If I were literate, my family and I would never be in slavery and I would not have lost my daughter." He explained that his employers took thumb impressions on papers against any amount of money, which he could never read and understand, pushing him into perpetual slavery. This is not just one family but the reality of millions trapped in slavery even in the 21st century only because they are illiterate.

The world is not fit for them, not because these children are sinners, but because the vested interests of ruling elites have monopolised all the opportunities and deliberately do not leave any space for the world's poor children.

Freedom and learning are the two birthrights of every human being. Any activity that takes away these rights is a crime against nature and humanity. Whatever be the reason, if a child is compelled to work at the cost of his freedom and education, it is a shame. It is a shame on those who exploit, but a bigger shame on those who offer them fine words and empty promises. Nelson Mandela rightly challenged this, saying, "Will our legacy be more than a series of broken promises?"

2002 will be a historic year for the world's children if we only honour the promises we have already made to them. This is the year when over a hundred governments have to show concrete results in wiping out the scourge of child slavery and prostitution, and use of children in armed conflicts and other hazardous work. This is the year when the world community is committed to make the concrete and time-bound action plans to ensure Education for All goals. This is also the year when the industrialised countries have to keep their promises to mobilise additional resources to ensure free and quality education for all children in developing countries especially for girls.

I strongly recommend the following five measures, which could make the world really fit for all children :

- Free quality education for all as the key to social justice, equity and combating poverty.
- A greater share for poor in the world's income.
- Global trade with fairness.
- The growing loss of livelihoods and dignity can only be prevented by measures to safeguard and sustain the natural resources on which the poor people depend.
- Peace is everyone's right.

There has been strong campaigning that at least 0.1 per cent of the rich countries' GDP should be committed for children from ODA. This is the least that the world can commit for them. This meager amount for them comes to $ 25-30 billion, which would be more than sufficient to ensure their freedom, health and education.

The present trend of global trade is marginalising the poor and taking away their land, livelihood, liberty and dignity. Children are becoming the worst victims of this unjust process. Not only that, hundreds of thousands of children are toiling in the production of goods for international market.

With regard to education, developing countries must meet their obligation to the people and to prepare credible, time-bound and concrete national action plans involving civil society by the end of 2002 as they promised in the World Education Forum in Dakar two years ago.

There must not be any levy on learning. Tuition fees, books, stationery and any expenses of schooling should be completely abolished in primary schools. The education should be of good quality, appropriate and relevant. More resources must be channeled to improve access and quality of public schooling available to the poorest children, disadvantaged communities and girls as well as other children in special circumstances, such as child labourers.

Last month, the world's finance and development ministers endorsed an EFA Action Plan to mobilise the additional resources needed to provide every child with free, quality primary education.

The countries like the Netherlands, Germany and the World Bank must be commended for announcing that they will back this plan with substantially increased financing for basic education. US and Canada have also committed to increase aid to education, and they are called on to endorse the EFA Action Plan, which represents the best chance in welcoming a generation of children fully enjoying their rights to education. This single and comprehensive plan of action will channel support to governments' own national strategies, rather than fragmenting efforts or imposing more conditionalities.

The leaders of the North will be in Canada next month when the G7 Finance Ministers meet in Halifax, and when G8 Heads of State gather in Kananaskis. The children of the South will be watching them. Too often the G8 has filled its communiqués with platitudes while dishing out media-friendly mini-initiatives. The success or failure of the G8 Summit will be judged on whether it delivers major and additional resources to support the EFA Action Plan, and pledges to immediately fill the financing gap in at least

20 countries that are strongly committed to providing quality education for every child.

I am not prepared to believe that the world is so poor that it cannot ensure freedom and education for its children.

Only $ 10 billion a year is needed for universal basic education. It is only 0.02 per cent of global income, or four days of military spending.

What we need now is political will. We want action today, and now.

❑

30

G-20 Leaders: Please Invest in Our Children

We need $ 40 billion to educate every child — your nations collectively spend 50 times that amount on the military.

You must invest more time, energy and capital on our true inheritors — the children of this world.

There is little doubt that the world we inhabit faces momentous challenges. There is no doubt whatsoever that you, representing the 20 most populous and powerful nations, have the power and can display the purpose to craft meaningful solutions. I am sure all of you are keen to work towards a better world where our most precious and valuable assets, our children, enjoy the freedom to chase their dreams. I strongly urge you not to forget children and the legacy we are leaving behind for them even as we wrestle with geopolitics.

"No country or community can lay exclusive claim to children. They are a shared global responsibility and legacy in the making."

More than the meek, it is the children who will inherit the Earth. No country or community can lay exclusive claim to children. They are a shared global responsibility and legacy in the making. It is children who will bear testimony if our efforts directed at sustainable growth have succeeded or not. Let us not let them down.

About two years ago, in Stockholm, I met laureates of different disciplines and spoke with them about the plight of children in slavery. They were deeply saddened and in disbelief. "Is it happening even today, Kailash? Are children really being bought and sold for prices lower than that for animals?" The conversation was very emotional. I could sense their compassion and the will to work for children. You, our leaders, too need to muster the same will and compassion.

Even as you gather in Hamburg, let me remind you that more than 5.5 million children are still living as modern-day slaves. What else can be more disgraceful and what else can be a more momentous challenge for global leaders? There is more to be ashamed of and to reawaken our collective conscience. More than 60 million children of primary school age are still denied their fundamental right of access to education and close to 170 million are still forced to work as child labour. How can this planet have a better future if the future of these children remains blighted?

Civil wars, interminable conflicts and natural as well as man-made disasters have made life a living hell for tens of millions of children, not to speak of the millions who have perished. According to a recent UNICEF report, about 50 million children have become refugees because of violence and conflict. Almost half of them come from Syria and Afghanistan. The number of refugee children has doubled in the last one decade. This has encouraged criminal gangs to indulge in child trafficking and slavery with even more impunity. More than half a million children are being trafficked and sold as sex slaves or bonded labour every year. There is a deeply disturbing trend of children being forced into conflict as combatants, suicide bombers and human shields. This reflects a complete disregard for basic tenets of humanity.

"You know well that education is the magic wand for children. If we genuinely believe in equality and in globalisation of compassion, every child must get access to education."

This has to stop. We, who have been raising our voices against abuse and exploitation of children and demanding access to education for them for decades, have achieved a lot. Just a few months ago, the World Summit of Peace Laureates was organised in Bogota, Colombia. One of our collective declarations was to: *"Call on all sectors to advance concerted action to end human trafficking, modern-day slavery, sexual exploitation, child labour and violence in all its forms against women and children."* About seven months ago, a global meeting of laureates and leaders organised in Delhi, led to the drafting of the Will For Children. Two years ago, in a historic move, the United Nations included an agenda for children while mapping the 17 Sustainable Goals of Development to be achieved by 2030. More than 180 member countries of the International Labour Organisation have ratified Convention 182 which prohibits the worst forms of child labour.

We have collectively achieved much, but much more needs to be done. If every child must get access to education by 2030, we have to completely eradicate child slavery and trafficking. I constantly dream that ours will be the last generation to witness child slavery and labour. Our children, and our collective future, need your intervention. The time is now. Right now.

Educated children create richer nations which are also healthier. Paying obeisance at the altar of GDP also demands universal education for children.

You know well that education is the magic wand for children. If we genuinely believe in equality and in globalisation of compassion, every child must get access to education. It is our moral commandment. You know how education can magically alter economic outcomes in this age of information and the Internet. Educated children create richer nations which are also healthier. Paying obeisance at the altar of GDP also demands universal education for children.

And do ponder over this: Just about $ 40 billion is needed to ensure every child in this world gets access to education. The 20 nations that you represent spend 50 times that amount every year on the military.

❑

31

I am Marching on a Bharat Yatra to Make India Safe again for Children

Let's declare war on child sexual abuse and trafficking. Today, I declare a war on child sexual abuse and trafficking. Today I am announcing Bharat Yatra, the biggest movement in history to make India safe again for children. I refuse to accept that the innocence, smiles and freedom of our children can keep getting stripped and violated. I refuse to accept that victims and ordinary people live in fear while perpetrators roam free and fearless. These are not ordinary crimes. This is a moral epidemic haunting our nation and the world.

This Bharat Yatra will be launched from Kanyakumari on 11 September 2017.

Just a few days ago, my wife Sumedha and I met five-year-old Salma (all names changed) in a hospital. She was raped by the van driver on her way back from school. Now, she trembles with fear at the mere mention of school. After a long chat with us, Salma pointed towards a lady doctor and whispered, "I want to be like her. She saved me." In Chandigarh, 13-year-old Rachna was going towards her school on 15 August to celebrate Independence Day. She was stalked, waylaid and raped. Her father asks, "Is this how my daughter and our family will remember Independence Day?" I also happened to meet a man whose 12-year-old son Naveen was repeatedly sexually assaulted by a relative over many months. Feeling degraded and ashamed to speak out, Naveen committed suicide. Today, the man asks, "For how long will we keep sacrificing our children at the sham altars of social stigma and family pride?"

"My aim is to inspire and provoke at least 10 million citizens to take the pledge for Surakshit Bachpan, Surakshit Bharat."

Today morning, I met the parents of Gudiya who was gangraped and murdered near Shimla. Talking to them was like staring at a haunted mirror. Each teardrop coming out of their eyes was a stinging indictment of our religions, our culture, our civilisation and our Constitution. The bereaved father told me, "Even you are a father. I pray and hope no father has to do what I did — pick up the naked dead body of my daughter that was riddled with cigarette burns. It was like she had been bitten by ravaging wolves. I couldn't save my daughter, but I am ready to do anything to save other children."

Dear friends, I will leave no stone unturned in my effort to reawaken the slumbering conscience of this nation. For the last many months, I have knocked at innumerable doors. I have personally met the President, Vice-President, Prime Minister, Union Ministers, many Chief Ministers, parliamentarians, faith leaders, entrepreneurs, judicial officers, child rights commissions, police officers as well as leading lights of education and social reform and they have come forth to support the movement. My aim is to inspire and provoke at least 10 million citizens to take the pledge for Surakshit Bachpan, Surakshit Bharat. We will also collectively demand that our Parliament passes a strong and effective law against trafficking.

I have organised and led many Yatras, where millions have joined me and marched alongside. These Yatras led to strict national and international laws against child labour. They also led to an amendment of the Constitution that made education a fundamental right. Many thought that I would lead a comfortable retired life after the Nobel Prize, but no, my dear friends, I am all set to march again. I call upon you to join the Bharat Yatra to make India safe again.*

❑

* Through this impassioned write-up, the author announced the formal launch of the historic Bharat Yatra against child sexual abuse and trafficking.

32

The Children of Crisis

The city of Istanbul in Turkey will witness an important development this week. For the first time ever, the international community will come together here for the World Humanitarian Summit on 23-24 May 2016 to discuss the serious humanitarian crisis that the world is facing.

Apart from challenges, such as climate change, terrorism, economic slowdown, unemployment and more, the biggest emergency facing us today is population displacement, migration and refugee crisis owing to insurgencies, conflicts, wars and natural disasters.

Today, one out of every seven persons lives in a conflict-ridden area. Almost half of the one billion crises-affected population of the world are children aged between three and 18.

"According to police reports, 10,000 refugee kids went missing in Europe. I ask where are these children?"

Some of the major consequences of conflict are separation of families, lack of opportunities in the formal labour market, increased poverty and greater chances of children going missing and becoming invisible. According to police reports, 10,000 refugee kids went missing in Europe. I ask where are these children? Are these invisible children forced into the worst forms of child labour and slavery? Unfortunately, the reality is that because of their vulnerability, children in such difficult times become the worst sufferers.

Both natural as well as man-created emergencies magnify the factors that increase children's vulnerability. Often, disasters such as earthquakes, floods and landslides propel children into child labour, early marriage and trafficking. It has been observed that post the insufficient aid disbursement in neighbouring Nepal after the brutal earthquake, there has been a spurt in child labour and trafficking cases. Similarly, the ongoing drought crisis in India is triggering internal displacement.

In fact, 184 million people were displaced by disasters in the world between 2008 and 2014. This is equivalent to a shocking one person per second.

As an immediate consequence of large-scale displacement, the education of an entire generation of children in several countries is being compromised. Almost half of the world's 59 million out-of-school children live in conflict areas. The education situation in humanitarian emergencies is even more sombre for girls, who are more than twice as likely as boys to drop out of school in such situations. In 2015 alone, 39 million girls had their education disrupted by emergencies.

"In Syria, young girls were sold for sex slavery for a price less than that of a pack of cigarettes."

In October 2015, I visited a Syrian refugee camp in Germany, where I met a child who had lost his leg and was confined to a wheelchair. This boy had seen his father get killed in a bomb attack in front of him. He had lost his mother on the way from Syria to Germany and had no family left. Still he told me that he would be delighted to go back to his home country if given security and education.

He was at least fortunate to survive — many of his brothers and sisters in similarly ravaged countries face a worse fate. In Syria, young girls were sold for sex slavery for a price less than that of a pack of cigarettes. On the Iraq-Syria border, a mere five-year-old child was given a gun by a militia group; when he failed to handle the gun, he was buried alive. A young girl forced into sexual slavery was killed when she was unable to satisfy her "customers".

It is our duty and responsibility as citizens of a humane, civilised world to stop this brutality on innocent young lives. *"Every heart and every door should be open to children. Not one more child should be left to suffer."*

The United Nations has identified seven pertinent areas that require immediate social, political and economic intervention:

- Prevent and end conflict.
- Respect rules of war.
- Leave no one behind.
- Catalyse action for gender equality.
- Respond to disasters and climate change.
- Work differently to end need.
- Invest in humanity.

At the summit, the Kailash Satyarthi Children's Foundation, along with our partners, will bring together leaders at a discussion on protecting children. Through a high-level panel, we will aim to build a strong political will to bring the issues of child labour, slavery and deprivation from education during crises, into the mainstream humanitarian response mechanism.

For steering out of the multi-faceted crises, several targeted national and international programmes are needed to reach those left furthest behind, such as displaced and refugee children engaged in the worst forms of child labour, or at risk of trafficking.

Gaps in education for children and youth must be eliminated for enabling them to secure a better future.

"Less than 2 per cent of all humanitarian aid was spent on education in 2015; this ought to change."

A strong legal support system for children in crises should be created along with raising awareness of the possible risks they might face. An increased onus lies on countries and communities to review and adapt national policies and budgets for providing better services to vulnerable children. Also, decriminalising of migration in such sensitive times can be explored. The focus also has to include long-term planned funding for victims and survivors of conflicts and disasters, apart from the provision of immediate relief.

We cannot afford to fail any more generations to the worst humanitarian crises ever.* With a sense of urgency, I will demand that not even one child is left unprotected. The humanitarian response mechanism ensures that children are not pushed into slavery, get trafficked or are forced to miss education. I appeal to governments, inter-governmental agencies, corporations and civil society for a concerted, coordinated, holistic and sustainable response.

"I commit to launch a worldwide youth campaign this year...to engage 100 million children and youth to champion the cause of approximately 100 million left-out young people."

A novel and positive element of this summit is that the participants are asked to make concrete political, financial or social commitments. Kailash Satyarthi Children's Foundation and I commit to launch a worldwide youth campaign this year for globalising compassion and inspiring global citizenship. This will aim to engage 100 million children and youth to champion the cause of approximately 100 million left-out young people. Simultaneously, we will launch an extraordinary initiative of Nobel Laureates and world leaders as a collective strong moral voice and force for children. The future belongs to our children and we must step up to the plate with funding so that no child is denied a childhood where they are free to be children, get an education and hope for a better future.

❑

* In this detailed piece, the author highlights the humanitarian crisis triggered by civil conflict and refugees and asks the world to pay more attention.

33

Laureates and Leaders Unite Because the Children cannot Wait Any Longer

On the 10th of December, a date celebrated as International Human Rights Day, as well as day of the annual Nobel Prize ceremony, a powerful moral voice rose from the highest pulpit of India, the Rashtrapati Bhavan in New Delhi. A gathering such as this one had never taken place before.

Twenty-five Nobel Laureates and global leaders assembled, with a strong resolve to put an end to the sufferings of children everywhere at the inaugural Laureates and Leaders for Children Summit.

"We live in a world full of children, but deprived of childhoods."

Independent attempts had been made across the world towards a common future where every child would be free, safe, healthy and educated. However, an intervention was required at the highest level: 168 million children work as labourers and 5.5 million are caught in slavery. One in seven children does not go to school. In India, every eight minutes a child goes missing. The global figure is unknown. In conflict-ridden countries, such as Syria, Palestine and South Sudan, about 21 million children are displaced and face inhumane conditions.

We live in a world full of children, but deprived of childhood. Our world today is wealthier than ever before, yet millions remain impoverished and in the margins of society. Leaps in education and technology have been unprecedented, yet millions are hard to reach and illiterate. Till the day the monopoly of the rich ends and poor children are no longer made victims of hasty development policies, we will continue to live in a disparate world.

I remember, after receiving my [Nobel] prize in Oslo, I was invited to interact with the laureates of other disciplines. When I shared narratives of the work we do and the cause we fight for, they were taken aback. Many of them were in utter disbelief. Some said, "Is it happening today, Kailash? Didn't slavery get abolished in the 19th century?"

The discussion brought tears to our eyes. I could feel the compassion in the room and their will to work for children. Since then, I've been mulling over ways to channelise the potential of these authorities of different disciplines for the most deprived children. I was also honoured to have had friends in some of the world leaders who were able to join us. In this fight against the abuse of children, we could not have missed out on the most powerful constituency of world leaders.

"At the Laureates and Leaders Summit, we gathered with one mission, to unite the world through compassion for our children."

At the Laureates and Leaders Summit, we gathered with one mission — to unite the world through compassion for our children. We assembled to find common solutions to our common problems, to tackle the issues of violence and neglect of children in policies.

The Hon'ble President of India, Shri Pranab Mukherjee, addressing the inaugural session, stated that it was a shared responsibility of all and a moral obligation to give children an equal opportunity. Calling it a 'noble task', he persuaded the leaders to commit themselves to the service of children.

The need of collective efforts has never been so dire. Prince Ali Bin Al Hussein of Jordan urged the world to recognise the plight of children caught in conflict zones.

Princess Charlene of Monaco emphasised that children must participate in decisions affecting them and the world needs to invest more to empower and equip them with knowledge of their rights. Princess Laurentien of the kingdom of the Netherlands called for changing the mindset of society towards children and His Holiness the Dalai Lama gave the clarion call to make the 21st century a century of peace and compassion.

"Imthiyaz, 16, asked the most pertinent question, which left us all shaken, 'How much longer are we to wait?'

Everyone present raised their voice, but the strongest voice was that of 16-year-old Imthiyaz Ali. He was enslaved at a garment factory in New Delhi and would routinely get beaten up by his employer. Activists of 'Bachpan Bachao Andolan' rescued him a few years ago and now he stays at our Bal Ashram in Viratnagar, Rajasthan.

Imthiyaz asked the most pertinent question, which left us all shaken, "How much longer are we to wait?"

Made stronger by the presence of the First Lady of Panama HE Lorena Castillo de Varela, former Prime Minister of Australia Julia Gillard, Madam Kerry Kennedy, Senator Tom Harkin (retired), Secretary General of the OECD Mr Angel Gurria and Nobel Peace laureates HE José Ramos-Horta, Madam Leymah Gbowee and Madam Tawakkol Karman, the summit progressed towards the idea of a united future by way of leaving behind a legacy, an individual and collective *Will for Children.*

Those gathered have promised to use their voices to protect the voiceless and marginalised children everywhere. We will take action and work towards a common goal of eradication in child labour in all its forms, and getting all our children into schools and encourage processes that will help monitor and uplift the progress made through relevant and robust metrics.

We will make efforts to prevent and end violence against children, and their exploitation in acts of terror and violence. We will support and encourage governments, inter-governmental organisations and the private sector to prioritise the empowerment of all children — including free, quality, public education, inclusive, affordable and equitable healthcare; protection, safety and well-being in their policies, business practices (especially supply chain behaviour) and financing.

"It is not our children who need us most, but it is we who rely on them to correct the wrongs of our society."

The world community now has targets against child labour, forced labour, modern slavery and human trafficking. This is an opportunity to embrace peace, equality and inclusivity by ensuring freedom for all children and it is not the duty of a few international agencies, or governments. It is the responsibility of each and every one of us, the corporate, civil society, media and citizenry. We must all raise our collective voice because children cannot wait.

Besides, it is not our children who need us most, but it is we, who rely on them, to correct the wrongs of our society and bring it to a more compassionate, progressive and resilient path of peaceful and sustainable development. Therefore, on the second day of the summit, we launched the '100 Million for 100 Million' campaign, which aims to harness the power of youth to act as leaders and change-makers on behalf of children worldwide.

In the meanwhile, I wish that the dream we dreamed together here, in New Delhi, begins to take form and children everywhere are allowed to enjoy their childhood and be free to be children.*

❑

---

* This was written when Kailash Satyarthi Children's Foundation organised the first Laureates and Leaders Summit in New Delhi in 2016.

34
Young People can Help Stop Slavery

The last year has seen such blatant violations of children's rights that instead of being shocked, the international community has sadly begun to accept these abuses as normal.

We have seen how thousands of Nepalese girls, forced on to the streets after the Nepal earthquake, have been trafficked into India and even possibly sold into the United Kingdom. Gross abuses, including rape, have been reported in Iraq. We have heard, first hand, how Syrian refugee girls as young as eight and nine have been forced into working for exploitative employers when they should be at school. And the plight of the girls kidnapped by Boko Haram from their school two years ago in Nigeria's Borno province continues to haunt us.

This month the Global Citizenship Commission, which reports to the UN Secretary-General, will call for a renewed commitment to ending slavery among young children. Modern slavery has permeated every aspect of our lives. Adults and children, many of them young girls, are being trafficked within and across countries to work in farms, factories or workshops. A recent report shows that there is a shocking rise in the number of children being used in suicide bombs.

"Instead of being shocked, the international community has sadly begun to accept these abuses as normal."

Modern forms of slavery take hold where there is conflict and corruption, and where there is systematic discrimination and inequality. With 60 million people displaced from their homes, levels of displacement due to conflict are at an all-time high and it means increased competition for low-paying jobs, but also more child labour, more children forced into begging on the streets and more girls forced into early marriage, with state authorities unable to prevent trafficking.

And while every country in the world except North Korea has laws that criminalise some form of slavery, human trafficking or forced labour, not all have credible and deliverable plans to do something about it.

While some countries have specialist security services and thousands of police, prosecutors and judges trained to respond to crime, far fewer countries have victim support services to rescue and rehabilitate victims of slavery and abuse. What's more, we have little experience of enforcing laws across borders to prevent the people, smugglers and criminal gangs who exploit and destroy young lives for profit.

Children work nearby to their parents at a construction project in front of Jawaharlal Nehru Stadium in New Delhi, India.

The Global Citizenship Commission has recently demanded an international criminal children's court to deal with cases of child abuse when national governments refuse to act. They have also recommended that the UN Security Council meet once every year as a children's council so that violations against children can be monitored, punished and prevented.

Business has a role to play in ending slavery, too. In 2016, President Obama closed loopholes in the US Tariff Act, 1930. The result is that no company can import into the United States goods made with forced or slave labour.

With the US Department of Labour maintaining an annually updated list of products produced by forced labour, already there is evidence of greater social responsibility among the business community. The UK's Modern Slavery Act, 2015 requires all companies with a turnover of more than 36 million GBP to report publicly on their efforts to ensure they are not using slave labour in their supply chains. *"Slavery cannot be combated with kid gloves."*

Modern slavery is an organised crime that requires the united might and will of all world leaders, businesses, and civil society to curb and combat it. We need robust policies that are adequately resourced and backed by effective enforcement with strong legal deterrents and economic sanctions where necessary.

What is new is a global civil rights struggle led by young people themselves against these modern forms of slavery. We know the difference that a campaign led by young people can make. The Global March Against Child Labour has highlighted the plight of 168 million children who are in child labour — and the 10 million school-age girls a year who are married off against their will. We need to give practical support to young people themselves in organisations like Girls Not Brides and the Global March Against Child Labour as they themselves stand up for their own rights. One of the Citizenship Commission's recommendations is long overdue — that every country has a youth Parliament that can meet to debate and campaign for young people and the services they need.

But it is education that makes the greatest difference. Getting children to school and registering their attendance is the biggest weapon against child labour, child marriage and child trafficking. And giving children an education offers the greatest opportunity for children to learn that slavery is evil. It also gives young people the hope that they can plan and prepare for their future. It is universal education that will spell the end of child slavery, and from the richest city of the richest country to the poorest slum and hovels of the developing world, we should unite in demanding an end to exploitation and universal education for all.*

❑

* In this inspirational write-up, the author calls upon the youth of the world to take the lead in eliminating slavery.

35

Ending the Business of Child Labour

In October 1997, when global leaders gathered in Oslo to strategise how to end child labour, we brought a huge ambition and a deep commitment to change. Through improved collaboration and planning, we sought to protect children from exploitation, and to develop "new strategies to eliminate child labour at the national, regional and international levels."

Now, 20 years later, it is time to ask: How have we done?

Poorly. Since that first meeting, the world has not even halved the number of children in the workforce. In the last five years, the international community has managed to reduce the number of employed children by just 16 million, the slowest pace of reduction in decades. Of the 152 million children working today, some 73 million are doing jobs considered hazardous. Even 'safe' child labour affects victims' physical and physiological well-being long into adulthood.

Worse, according to the most recent data from the International Labour Organisation, the world has made the least progress in protecting two of the most at-risk populations — children between the ages of five and 11, and young girls.

The problem is not that we have failed to learn anything during our four global gatherings (the most recent one, held in Buenos Aires, wrapped up earlier this month). The problem is that we have failed, and are failing, to take our own advice.

Even as we talk, disturbing global developments have added a sinister twist to child labour and trafficking. This was supposed to be the century of empowerment for the most marginalised. Instead, we are witnessing globalisation of the most perverted kind, with children becoming victims many times over.

Because traffickers can easily hunt amid chaos, children in conflict zones are particularly vulnerable. Syria has commanded attention for years because of the horrific violence to which children are subjected. But the global rise of organised gangs means that children in Asia, Africa, Latin America and Europe are also at risk. Stemming this trend requires urgent and coordinated investment in education and safety wherever children are at risk — in conflict zones, refugee camps and in areas affected by natural disasters.

I am often left wondering how we got to this point. Over the last 37 years, colleagues and I have rescued more than 87,000 children from forced labour in India. We have rescued girls who were so abused that they lost their ability to speak. Recently, we rescued children from a garment factory in New Delhi, where, for more than three years, they had been forced to sit and work for 20 hours a day in a basement with no ventilation. When they were brought to Mukti Ashram, our transit rehabilitation centre, many were unable to walk or even look up at the sun.

We are proud of our accomplishments. But human depravity is a source of continued sorrow.

How can we end this suffering once and for all? Global gatherings, like the one that just ended, certainly have a role to play, but talk alone will not suffice. Serious problems confronting humanity are tackled only when stakeholders become full participants.

Successes in public health are instructive. For example, there was a time when diseases like polio and smallpox ravaged millions. Through the coordinated efforts of doctors, volunteers, global institutions, local governments and civil society, these diseases were tamed. Similar collaboration is needed now to reduce child labour.

The first place to start is to target industries where child labour is present, such as agriculture. In addition to strong legal frameworks, robust accountability mechanisms must be established to guarantee that child labour is not used in supply chains. I have found that with the right incentives, businesses and consumers can become partners in eradicating child labour.*

One example of this collaboration emerged from the carpet industry in South Asia, where children were being mercilessly exploited. To force change, we launched a movement to educate consumers in the West to compel carpet factory owners to behave responsibly. This led to the creation of a label, GoodWeave, which certifies that no child has been put to work in manufacturing the product. Since the label was launched more than 20 years ago, child labour in the region's carpet industry has plummeted, from roughly one million to about 200,000.

Programmes like these are helpful, but the most important changes must come from international efforts led by the United Nations. Ending the vicious circle of child labour, illiteracy and poverty will require intergovernmental agencies to come together around each of the sustainable development goals that directly affect children. These include Goal 8, ending forced labour, modern slavery, trafficking and child labour; Goal 4, ensuring education for all; Goal 3, providing universal access to healthcare; and Goal 16, stopping all forms of violence against children.

To succeed, UN Secretary-General António Guterres will need to channel more resources towards improving children's lives. His first course of action should be to call

---

* In this heartfelt appeal to the world, the author points out how child labour continues to haunt and torment the world.

a meeting with the heads of UN agencies and international organisations, as well as world leaders, to create an agenda for concerted and coordinated efforts to protect young people everywhere.

At the end of the day, only political will can disrupt the grim calculus of child labour. We cannot build a more peaceful, sustainable world without ensuring the freedom, safety and education of every child. A life of work robs children of all three.

As I ponder the way forward, I cannot forget a young girl I met in Brazil, whose small hands were horribly injured and bleeding from plucking oranges. She asked me a simple question, to which I did not have an answer: "How can the world enjoy the juice from these oranges when children like me have to shed their blood to pluck them?"

That is a question we all must ask ourselves, too.

❑

36

The Human Right that Keeps on Giving

In Côte d'Ivoire, I once met a boy working on a cocoa farm whose only dream was someday to taste the rich brown chocolate he helped produce. And in Pakistan, I once rescued a boy who sewed footballs and wished only to play with the product of his work.

In the course of more than three decades of defending children's rights — including rescuing tens of thousands of children from bonded labour and slavery, among them little girls who were trafficked from their homeland for sexual exploitation — I have met young people from many backgrounds. But, whether they are child labourers or victims of war who have lost everything, all have something in common — an indomitable urge to study. They want nothing more than to pick up a book, go to school and improve their lives through education.

According to UNESCO, every additional year of schooling a young person receives increases their average future earnings by 10 per cent, and can boost countries' average annual GDP growth by 0.37 per cent. Education doesn't only break the shackles of human slavery; it can also fuel social, economic and political changes.

❑

37

Winning the War on Child Sexual Abuse

With every new crisis that the world faces, humanity's differences appear increasingly intractable. Religion, ethnicity, history, politics and economics have all become tools to denigrate and demean. People seem to be drifting apart, and no country is immune from divisive discourse.

But there is one fundamental issue where contrasts dissolve into consensus: the desire to keep children safe. Protecting the physical, emotional and psychological well-being of children is a universal instinct that no faith, dogma, or ideology can defeat. And yet, despite this shared instinct, children everywhere continue to be preyed upon. Too often, societies ignore child sexual abuse owing to family pride or fear of stigma. The world can stay silent no longer.

The numbers are truly alarming. According to a 2016 World Health Organisation report, one of every four adults was sexually abused as a child. A 2007 Indian Government study found that 53 per cent of children in India faced some form of sexual abuse growing up. And human trafficking, especially trafficking of children, is a booming business, with annual average profits totalling $ 150 billion. In other words, child sexual abuse is a moral epidemic afflicting the entire world — one that we can defeat only when we openly declare war against it.

❑

38

From Child Slavery to Freedom

It is a blot on the face of humanity that we have yet to eradicate slavery of children, no less. Not only does child slavery persist, the number of child slaves, 5.5 million, has remained constant in the last two decades. They are bought and sold like animals, sometimes for less than a pack of cigarettes. Add to their number the 168 million child labourers, 59 million out-of-school children and 15 million girls under 15 who are forced to marry every year and the situation is beyond unacceptable.

Eighteen years ago, the Global March Against Child Labour spearheaded a global movement to bring child labour and child slavery to the attention of global leaders. Thanks to the invaluable contribution of fellow activists, workers, educators and businesses, the campaign was a resounding success, leading to the adoption of the International Labour Organisation's Worst Forms of Child Labour Convention.

Clearly, however, there is much work left to do. That is why, the Global March Against Child Labour worked so hard — collecting 550,000 signatures on a petition — to push world leaders to include strong language against child slavery in the sustainable development goals, which will guide global development efforts for the next 15 years. Among the SDG targets is one that aims to "eradicate forced labour, end modern slavery and human trafficking, and secure the prohibition and elimination of the worst forms of child labour."

❑

39

Business Solutions to End Child Labour and Slavery

Two days ago, the global society got together to celebrate the World Day Against Child Labour. But, on this joyous occasion, I was caught between varying emotions. On the one hand, I feel a sense of accomplishment that the issue is being globally deliberated upon, but on the other, I am still reminded of 168 million child labourers we are yet to reach. About 5.5 million of those children are engaged in modern forms of slavery, and 85 million work in worst forms of child labour.

We are a world in crisis — a proliferation of natural and man-made disasters, and conflicts and insurgencies has put incredible strain on the well-being of children. The earthquake in Nepal last year, the drought in India, the forever-prevalent crisis in Africa and the most inhumane conflict in Syria have all revealed concrete evidence of children being trafficked for slavery, sexual exploitation and labour. Due to our inability to confront disasters and the lack of post-disaster humanitarian assistance, an increase in school drop-out rates and child labour has been witnessed in the affected areas. The recent cases of Syrian children working in Turkish garment factories, children from Nepal being trafficked into UK, or the rising incidences of child marriages threaten to overturn the gains from last decades.

Business-as-usual will buckle under sustained pressure from these crises. And, under duress, the world community must collectively engage to find solutions, reflecting and innovating for sustainable change and development. Furthermore, the process of globalisation and other global developments over the past decades have seen non-state actors, such as transnational corporations and businesses, play an increasingly important role not only internationally, but also at the national and local levels.

More and more companies have recognised that they must operate responsibly and work to uphold international agreements on human rights, especially zero tolerance towards child labour and slavery, in their supply chains. However, in recent times there is a growing awareness that the goods and services supply chains are not immune to the presence of child labour. Of all the exploited people, children are the most vulnerable, physically, mentally and emotionally.

While 'corporate social responsibility' efforts have reached a critical point in time, with much learning and improvement, there is still much to be accomplished. In the 90s, when I was rescuing children from the carpets there was no 'corporate social responsibility' and 'social labelling' came into existence with our efforts for child labour-free carpets. Since then, we have come a long way, yet the current prevalent system hinges on 'policing'. There are more children, women and men in slavery now than at any time in world's history. Greater accountability and transparency clubbed with real stakeholder engagement should be at the core of ethical business.

This approach has been manifest in a number of initiatives around the world, from carpets, football stitching, garments, cocoa, mica, etc. which have experienced varying degrees of success.

Vasu Marandi (name changed) from Kanichiyar in Jharkhand, a scrawny boy, 12 years of age, the head of children's assembly in his village walked down to school with his schoolmates protesting teachers' quality. Several years back, before 'Bachpan Bachao Andolan' started working in the heartland of Naxal activities, there were thousands of Vasus toiling in the mica mines, dreaming of an education. Mica is the glitter in the cosmetics and most sought after in the electronic industry as a non-conductor of electricity. It was also the cause of empty schools and rampant child labour in these villages. Through the *Bal Mitra Gram* programme, we have withdrawn more than 4,000 children from child labour and enrolled in school, and we work directly with over 15,000. The traders are being sensitised, the big transnational corporations are beginning to look deeper into their supply chains, and the administration is more engaged. At the heart of it is the empowerment of children and the community.

In the wake of widespread child labour and human rights abuse in the lower levels of global supply chains of some prominent apparel brands, Global March Against Child Labour convened multi-stakeholder initiative involving major actors in the garment supply chain, including all the manufacturers and sub-contractors. Holistic approach was made to reach all vulnerable points — from deprived and impoverished communities at risk of trafficking, to the unorganised workers and not-recognised sub-contractors, through this initiative.

It is time we rise above our traditional and conventional thinking in these linkages since a minute late is a minute too late. A comprehensive policy and legislative framework, set within efforts to bring social change, is paramount. But the same vision has to apply to the issue of how business practices can impact child labour.

The need of the hour is business with compassionate intelligence. Business with intelligence is a common thing but business with compassionate intelligence will have a different notion. Compassion is key in business. It is the compassion that will bring about a magical leadership, will transform from traditional thinking to innovative solutions, where communities are seen as stakeholders and not consumers.

As we mark June 12 and commemorate the hundreds of thousands of marchers of the Global March Against Child Labour (1998), and remember the call 'From Exploitation to Education', we look upon the business sector to ensure that their supply chains are free from child labour and slavery. Remember, those who suffer the most from society's existing defects stand to gain the most from social reforms.*

This year, let us not disappoint our children.

❑

* In this penetrating analysis, the author shows how entrepreneurs and business enterprises can become partners in abolishing child labour and slavery.

INTERVIEWS

INTERVIEWS

1

'Biggest Challenge is to Break Silence on Child Sexual Abuse'

A crusader against child labour, Nobel laureate Kailash Satyarthi now takes up preventing child sexual abuse as his mission.

On a visit to the city as part of his Bharat Yatra campaign for child safety and against child trafficking, Nobel Peace Prize laureate Kailash Satyarthi talks to The Hindu *about the taboo on speaking out against child abuse and how society is not prepared to make use of a strong law like the Protection of Children from Sexual Offences (POCSO) Act, because while the law is good, enforcement by judicial institutions is necessary.*

Do you think child sexual abuse has become such an important issue that you had to take out a Yatra?

This menace of child sexual abuse, rape, violence against children and child trafficking is growing and has become a moral epidemic. The entire society is affected by it, whether it is a boy or a girl, rich or poor, it is prevalent in big cities and small. Children are not safe in schools, at home and in public spaces. Sadly, in most cases, they don't speak up under the garb of honour, respect and dignity, because we don't have the environment where children can vent. They live in depression and frustration, which affects their personality. In many cases, the abuse is done by their own relatives, and the biggest challenge is to break the silence.

Children and parents, the entire society, need to break the silence surrounding it. Otherwise, it is soon going to ruin the family and value system. Not only children, but parents are also afraid of relatives. This is a fight against fear, to bring in freedom of mind.

What do you think we can do to curb the number of cases?

One way is by what we are doing, that is, by mass awareness. Whether it is the government, private sector or religious institutions, we are trying to explore their roles, which has never been done before. Because compassion for children is the only thing that can bring everyone together and mitigate differences.

Do you think cases of child sexual abuse have increased in recent years?

There has been an increase in cases, but also an increase in cases reported, so that is good news. At least we are talking about them. Ten years ago, a report by the United Nations Educational, Scientific and Cultural Organisation and the Government of India said 53 per cent of Indian kids are sexually abused, which means one in two children is abused. But many times, they don't know what happened; they feel uncomfortable. Nowadays, they know that it is a bad touch, but they don't know it is sexual abuse. And, secondly, they don't speak out and don't tell their parents, and, hence, cases go unreported. Therefore, we just had 15,000 cases reported in millions.

Do you think we have enough laws to deal with child sexual abuse?

Law is important, and it is like a tool, like a weapon. But when you don't have the courage and the mind to use it, it's of no use as the society is not prepared to use the weapon. Society is not prepared to use a strong law like the POCSO Act. The Act is very good in itself, but enforcement has to take place through judicial institutions, as prosecution is not taking place and the conversion of prosecution to conviction is minimal.

Another problem is victims and their families live with a social taboo; they live in fear and predators move around freely. I came across a man whose two daughters, aged three and 17, were raped by the neighbour. He got bail after a few months, and in that small locality, he roamed around freely. The girls were traumatised as they had to look at his face every day. This compelled the father to send them to their native place.

What do you think is the reason for not getting enough convictions?

We don't have the judicial infrastructure for the POCSO Act. The judge in the designated POCSO court is also dealing with other responsibilities and cases. Designated doesn't mean anything; in my view, we need exclusive. The problem will be solved only when we have a designated court to try crimes against children in every district. That judge has to be properly trained and sensitised. There has to be psychological support infrastructure. The designated police officers have to be sensitised so that they can deal with such cases. We need to bring in accountability and cases have to be dealt with in a time-bound manner. But, most importantly, the mindset has to change.

❑

2

The World Needs to Become More Aware

Well-known media personality and anchor Arnab Goswami who was then with Times Now *asked a series of questions from Nobel Peace Prize winner in an exlusive interview.*

People crave for Nobel Prize. What was your reaction when you got the prize?

I was surprised to hear my name. I had no idea that Nobel Peace Prize will be declared on this day. I was checking the flight tickets for my trip to Germany and was unaware of the prize.

How is life after Nobel?

We are working on some brilliant projects right now. After Nobel, I received a lot of national and international media attention.

Does it upset you that you are being recognised in your country only after you got international fame?

I work for invisibility, for people and children who are invisible but work very hard. My time and energy is for people who work very hard. When I visit different states and meet kids and their parents, I feel extremely happy.

Were politicians supporting you when you didn't win Nobel?

Unfortunately not! These kids weren't on the political radar. Kids weren't voters; that's why the politicians didn't care much. The politicians didn't see any benefit in me. So, they ignored! But now, I see support from them.

Does this not make you sceptical of these politicians?

No, I welcome them, atleast they are awakening. Through me, they are talking about children. Each person who comes and congratulates me...I tell them this Nobel Prize is for every Indian. India has been waiting to get a Nobel since Mahatma Gandhi. I got Nobel Prize because of these children, not my effort. The voices of these children were never heard. Now people have started talking about these children.

Were you aware of reasons why Government of India wanted you to sit out of meetings? Why was government suspicious of you?

UNESCO leadership asked me questions on what are you going to speak? Illiteracy? I decided to speak about children who are deprived of education around the world.

Every Indian politician now wants to bask in your glory. Why was the government suspicious of you?

The government is the best to answer why. I was working with children who were trafficked, abused, children who were enslaved and bought at lesser prices than animals. We found out that many of these local mafias are so connected with the political and local authorities. I had nothing against politicians. I was just fighting against a crime that was intolerable. There were some politicians who were supportive too.

Please describe this picture where you are bleeding while trying to rescue girls from the circus.

We were going to protect these girls from a circus in UP where we were attacked by the circus authorities. We survived but it was horrifying. My daughter was also getting threats. We were suspicious that the local authorities were connected to the circus owner.

Where was your wife when you and your son were attacked?

She was in Bal Ashram in Jaipur, a child rehabilitation centre, and there was no connectivity there.

What you have done with 'Bachpan Bachao Andolan' is tremendous. It must have been a lonely and difficult journey as you have done it all alone? Even the government didn't support you then. Now after Nobel, things have changed. It's been almost three decades. Why did you choose to do this?

I was a great lover of freedom. I read about revolutionaries when I was small like Gandhi and Bal Gangadhar Tilak. There were no NGOs when I was small. I passed out as an engineer and worked for a year. The thought of doing something was always on my mind. Thousands of letters came from activists across the world when I received the Nobel. They feel like they got it. I feel happy to see them happy. These social workers are the pioneers.

In an interview, you spoke about how you rescued these children from the carpet industry? The carpet industry was run by influential people who are well connected. You have rescued children from this carpet industry which is also run by MPs and ministers. This is a serious issue.

I am not against these MPs. I am against the social evil.

Now that you have the power, would you name these MPs? If the Indian Government asks you to disclose these names confidentially, would you disclose their names?

We will ask the government to do something, a sincere investigation on all the blocks, in the areas where government officials live. Young girls who are trafficked by placement agencies should be rescued and lots of work needs to be done. India has a Nobel Prize now and it's everybody's moral responsibility to abide by the ethics and not encourage child labour.

Did former PM Chandra Shekhar threaten you?

We read in the newspapers that this child labour issue is nonsense in the carpet industry, PM Chandra Shekhar said. He said he will do his best to remove it from the industry if there's any child labour.

One former PM threatens to take action against you and one PM invites you for tea after Nobel? How has things changed?

PM Modi was really excited and constructive on the issue of child rights. It wasn't simply courtesy but his openness was really commendable.

Are NGOs trying to do something essentially anti-India and want to spoil the image of India internationally? The NDA Government views NGOs suspiciously. Do they represent Western interest? Do you think this suspicion is justified?

As far as I read in the papers and came to know from my NGO friends, it wasn't just in this government; it was done in the past governments too. It's just that it's coming out now.

There's a generalisation that the funding Indian NGOs receive is a part of discredit India campaign. They are ruining the great India story.

I would look at the purpose of the funding. What's the intention of the donor and receiver? The whole issue is of transparency in receiving and justifying the donation. We are accountable to the people whom we work with and work for. The moral component is a part of it. Civil society has a very important role as critical policy partners.

Criticism is that many activists hype problems in India for many reasons: Madhu Kishwar says only the activists who receive international funding get Nobel. Why does this kind of criticism come?

This is the perception of many and I won't comment on just one person. This is because of lack of information. They should gain information. There will be people with diverse opinions.

Where did you do your engineering from?

I did it in Vidisha. My mother sold her ornaments to make me study. She was worried and she cried when I left engineering. It was end of 80s. When I gave up, my mother was worried about my career and also my safety. I was not deterred by the tears of my mother, although tears had the power to deter me.

Do you feel child labour and human trafficking in India is a dirty secret that is not given much attention? And authorities are in denial about it. There's a conflict between authorities and activists in India. What's your stance? Maybe you can be the bridge?

This is something I knew right from the beginning and even now that this is a fight against the mindset. This is a fight against vested interest and old-age tradition and I knew who will be on the other side. A 100 people or more? I believe, in India, I was able to live and work because of democracy. Some of the best judgements came out of India's courts. The courts made the investigations and found hidden facts. In 1981, SC took the case of Asiad Village. The tradition of Indian judiciary has been enormous. I was telling my son today that the latest situation of missing children is so serious and severe. Fifteen children go missing every hour in India. These children are trafficked and they are bonded labourers. These facts come from the Indian Government and not from my organisation. The media has been very supportive throughout in bringing out these facts.

You have the power to shake things up. People now look up to you. You are an icon! You have rescued many children. There must be one image in your mind which stands with you when you thought you took the right decision?

Each time I rescue a child, I feel it's a small victory over slavery. I feel I am freed. I believe in inner emancipation and freedom. Freeing a child is a divine feeling. When a mother cries and tears of joy flow after seeing her child, I feel freed and lucky to experience the same. Let me share with you one story. We went to rescue stone-quarry workers in Haryana. The quarry belonged to a big politician in Haryana. His son was a Parliament member. Police weren't willing to go in. So, we waited the whole night and early morning; we rescued the group of around 50, children, men and women. In many cases, drivers run away or they are bribed. I was driving the car and others were in the truck. We found the kids were traumatised and scared. The quarry owners got these people. It was their third generation that was working there. These people were scared and were working there for years and years. These people had never seen a fruit in their life. They had been kept in poor conditions and given poor food. A lady asked me, "Why didn't you come early?" This question that I heard is for all those people who talk of humanity. There is a tremendous sense of urgency and we need to take action now! If you come to see any child is exploited, think what if that child was yours. Compassion has to be translated into action. We globalise market but we have to globalise compassion and sustain our society.

May there be thousands of Kailash Satyarthis. I respect and wish you success in all your endeavours.

I watch your shows with passion and it is this passion that connects me and you!

❑

3

Corporates should also Play an Important Role in Safeguarding the Interests of Children

Nobel laureate Kailash Satyarthi is spearheading a new campaign against child abuse. The activist plans to bring together on one platform a host of Nobel laureates from different fields. The objective — use their stature to win global support for the rights of children. Satyarthi believes that the state, corporates and the civil society must work hand in hand to ensure justice for the neglected and abused children across the world.

Edited excerpts from an interview with Business Today's *Anilesh Mahajan.*

We are all hearing about your new initiative 'Laureates and Leaders for Children'....

It is for the first time in history that a strong platform of Nobel laureates and world leaders is being created for the cause of children. We are calling it 'Laureates and Leaders for Children' and it is aimed at bringing these leaders together at India's Rashtrapati Bhawan. We have got support of 34 Nobel laureates from different disciplines and 14 will be joining here. But many of those who are not coming will send or have sent their video message. Several UN agency heads and some top children rights activists and some kings and queens would be also joining this initiative.

Simultaneously, we are also talking about a very ambitious and largest ever youth campaign, '100 Million for 100 Million'. We are trying to harness the energy and idealism of some 100 million youth who are better off in schools, colleges, universities and in the professional world. This would take up the cause of 100 million left-out children around the world. Around 100 million young people suffer violence, slavery, trafficking, prostitution, child marriage. Many of these are children who are forced to leave their country and become refugees. So, 100 million young people are going to connect with 100 million left-out children. This campaign will be launched on December 11 in India and that will be followed in many more countries in the coming months.

How are you going to arrange the required funds for these campaigns? Are some corporate houses bringing in some capital?

The whole idea is that corporates should also play an important role in safeguarding the interest of children globally and it means that we have to be more responsible and ensure that no child labour or trafficked child is involved in the supply chain and production activities anywhere. They should also ensure that wherever they are operating, they can help vulnerable, marginalised children through education, healthcare, immunisation social awareness, social empowerment, etc. They can also play an important role in protecting children. We invited a number of business leaders, as well as representatives of public sector undertakings from across the world. The conventional wisdom was that these are the responsibilities of the state but now in the last 20 years, two new sectors have emerged — one is the civil society and the other is the corporate world, with their own set of values. Civil societies have tremendous knowledge of and grassroots experience about social problems. Similarly, the corporate sector is not just a money-making machine; now their character is changing very fast. They have started to think of ecological issues, how to protect the environment and how to protect people. Hence, consider them equal stakeholders to safeguard not only the children but the planet and people at large. I call it 'business with compassionate intelligence'. Profits should be connected with people of the planet. That will be possible not only through conventional wisdom and intelligence but also by keeping in mind how to make this a happier world where your customers, your consumers, your workers, your management people and other stakeholders feel happy and not a sense of guilt at any stage. That would be a business with compassionate intelligence.

Do you think, in a way, the world is changing, with deglobalisation voices propping up? Do you think this is the right time for such efforts?

No, we have seen the impact of globalisation. There was globalisation of the economy and the markets and then technological growth. The technological growth was driven by fast data and digital transmission. So, that became the globalisation of information and knowledge. We have seen some good results as well as some drastic ones because of it. People are now trying to squeeze themselves into their own identity of nationalities, nationalism and things like that. It is opposite to the traditional globalisation thoughts. But you cannot stop globalisation but what you can do or what we are trying to do through these two initiatives is to bring 'globalisation of compassion'. The West has initiated the globalisation of the economy, which has its own ramifications and, learning from their experience, this is the right time to try 'globalisation of compassion'. Eventually, you will have to feel connected and it will make you more confident and fearless. Fear is manifested in many ways — the fear of losing a job, the fear of losing identity. It can be an outcome of Brexit and other events. It is necessary to create a different culture — globalisation of compassion. When we start feeling for others at a different or deeper level, it will help each other's needs.

But we also have seen that the last 20-25 years of globalisation also led to phases of exploitation. This included child labour, exploitation of labour through informal channels. So, do you think that this compassion model will help individual countries to rethink and change the way they operate?

Yes. This is precisely why we wanted to harness and channelise the power of youth. Simultaneously, we are trying to engage moral authorities from all walks of life, right from Nobel laureates to other thought leaders. The idea is to begin with the children. It's much more easier to get into the bigger debate thereafter. Children are non-controversial — nobody can say let children die of hunger, let the children face violence. No one can justify slavery or child rape.

What sort of role do you see the US playing under Donald Trump?

I would be definitely inviting him to take the lead in protecting children of his country and children globally. I know that hundreds and thousands of children are working in mining, agriculture, shops and other places in the US itself and they are facing hazardous situations dealing with machines, electricity, pesticides and chemicals. Trump has to do something for those children as well.

And what about refugees?

In case of refugees, I have been saying again and again that no purse, pockets or borders should be closed for children. No heart should be closed for children — children are the true reflection of God and humanity/human beings. We should not put any walls or barriers or borders for children. I am of the opinion that one day the world will get rid of these borders. By narrowing your minds and hearts, you are not allowing children to travel freely around the world.

Trump has won with an ultra-nationalist campaign...

Let him come. People in election campaigns use all kinds of populist measures and the masses follow them. But once they are elected, the seat has its own character and gravity. The seat of the President of the USA comes with its own set of powers and responsibilities and, so, whoever assumes office, will not be able to ignore the moral responsibility towards the country, the world. When he speaks of deportation of illegal immigrants, my biggest concern is the children. What is going to happen to the children who are born in the US to such immigrant parents? So, the government has to ensure justice, care and protection for those children.

And what about Europe? It is also going through turmoil.

Even in Europe, children should not suffer because of politics, measures or ideological factors. Children are not responsible. We have to create a safe world for them. Eventually, these very children are the custodians of the Earth. If we are not treating our custodians well, how can we say we are civilised?

China is also changing its economic policies. But we hardly know the fate and magnitude of the exploitation going on there. What are your apprehensions about child labour in that country? Will your group be working to bring a change there?

I don't think anybody has deep knowledge and understanding about the situation of child labour in China. except on a few occasions when media exposed it. Children were found working in some electronic factory...so, there definitely must be child labour but we need more concrete knowledge about it. China is also a part of the world and this moral platform is universal and the message will go across. We are not going to pressurise anyone as it is against the essence of this platform.

China has one-fifth population of the world and its voice is excluded...

Within China also we try to contact the Chinese youth and Chinese people. A big segment of young people are denied their rights and the voice must go across. Nowadays, you cannot stop any communication. Luckily, the social media and the web...

But they blocked Facebook, Twitter and other social media platforms...

Yes, but there are other ways. People are getting information through so many ways. The young people are doing business and have open minds. So, it's not possible to keep everything closed forever.

And what about India?

India has made considerable progress, no doubt about it. In many areas for children, like education, there has been substantial increase in enrolment, the number of child labourers has gone down, instances of child marriages are lesser than before. In spite of this progress, India being the largest democracy in the world, the most ancient civilisation, our moral responsibility and obligation are much more. And if I see that our girls are not safe — there are instances of girls sold at a lower price than animals — and we are unable to impart quality education to all our children, then I see these as big challenges. So, we have all stakeholders like the world of business, religious leaders and the government. We must work hand in hand to get rid of these crimes against children as these are still prevalent.

Can we see your platform helping governments in framing strategies for making laws?

Not laws. But we will encourage the establishment to promote pro-children policies and we will lend our voices and expertise in these areas and discipline to the government. And encourage intergovernmental agencies as well as the business sector to prioritise the issues related to children. We will be supporting all efforts and encourage positive steps towards this cause.

Any countries you have shortlisted, or any country that you want to go to first? How will this group actually work?

These details will be worked out when the laureates and leaders meet and form a consensus. We intend to meet every year, but would continuously engage with each other. If there are any emerging and pressing issues, we may react any time collectively. More or less, the moral authority and power of these Nobel laureates is still intact, people still have that respect. This authority has never been acknowledged or identified or harnessed for the cause of children.

When I share my experiences and issues related to children facing violence with Nobel laureates from different fields and disciplines, many of them get shocked. They don't come across these things or they never thought about these issues — these are the people who have devoted their whole life for knowledge sitting in labs, library and universities. They too are human beings, who also have a sense of idealism and feelings of compassion. They are like old saints who have been meditating for many years. Your intellectual powers and your research, your inventions and other accomplishments are well known and utilised by the world but what about the moral authority you possess? That is not really utilised. This they have realised because their voice cannot be ignored easily. If 20 to 50 Nobel laureates write a letter to any head of UN and similar agencies, it cannot be ignored. No President or PM can ignore them... that is my sense.

Many countries refuse to acknowledge that child marriage should be illegal. You will need to bring about change in these kinds of issues...

Yes, the politicians keep several considerations in mind, do not raise their voice and do not interfere in the affairs of others, but we can speak out loudly for those young people who are suffering. The moral platform will be working on this without any bias or any hesitation or fear.

I have been a part of several campaigns against child marriages in Pakistan, in Bangladesh, in India and also in some of the African countries on genital mutilation of girls but not with this platform. I'm part of such campaigns even now but let us see how these laureates and leaders react to it.

Is Malala Yousafzai also coming or part of this summit?

She is not coming. We have invited her but she is a student and is busy with her studies and, unfortunately, her examination is round the corner. She is like my daughter and even my wife has a very good rapport with her.

But she is an icon...

Let her complete education at least. She herself has understood that completing education is important. We have to keep that in our mind. We have a very good relationship with her and her family.

Do they (Nobel laureates) joining you also have a common agenda on children rights? For example, in Philippines, there are certain kinds of issues related to children and it would be different from Syria, etc...

Unfortunately, nobody is coming from Philippines but, yes, they are coming from the Middle East like Tawakkul Karman, who is representing Yemen. She is a bright young lady who is fighting violence against children, specially the refugees. Similarly, Nobel laureates from Tunisia are fighting for democracy and against autocracy. I am not sure that any of the Nobel laureates who is coming is solely working on the issues of children. I was the first to be conferred a Nobel for the cause of children. It never happened in 125 years of Nobel.

My last question is about demonetisation. How do you see this step helping in eradication of child labour?

I supported this because every single penny earned through human trafficking and child trafficking, child prostitution, slavery and child labour is black money. The whole chain of operations is managed with black money. So, the step has helped a lot (this big assault on black money). Not just crimes against children, any type of organised crimes happening in India or anywhere in the world through black money. Black money perpetuates crime. There is also a third angle and that is corruption. Organised crime cannot function without a corrupt government machinery. Corruption, black money and organised crime make a full circle. But to fully control organised crime, this is a good step but not enough because it is an ongoing activity. We are unable to make good laws and enforce them if our justice delivery system is not fast enough, if we don't have adequate number of judges. If we don't have all this in place, this issue will go on. Overall, it is a good move but it is one of the moves. We will have to plug other channels as well to have complete control on crime.

❑

4
Everybody has Globalised the Economy, Let's Globalise Compassion

Nobel Peace laureate Kailash Satyarthi is launching a global initiative with the highest moral authorities of the world — 25 Nobel laureates and world leaders — for the cause of children. It is for the first time that such revered personalities will assemble together on one platform on December 10 to give a clarion call for prioritising the issues of children in global, political and social discourse. He shares his 'child-friendly India' campaign with Rinku Ghosh.

How has the Nobel changed you from the days of the 'Bachpan Bachao Andolan'?

Now we have a better office (laughs). But jokes apart, we have much more to do than just field work. We have hired specialised researchers and analysts to process and interpret our findings and statistics and help set the template for the future course of action. Undoubtedly, our grassroot activists and on-ground workers fighting for the dignity and health of each underprivileged child are the real power. But our desk-foot soldiers are no less, collating and analysing data in such a manner that we can influence policies, not only nationally but internationally too. What are the loopholes in international policy? What could be done not only in India but across the world? For that, we need differently skilled people and, hence, we extended our office. You will still find me through at my old offices in Kalkaji.

I have not forgotten my moorings. (Introducing Om Prakash, retired GM, NTPC.) He was the only friend who trusted me when I gave up my engineering career in 1980 to campaign for child rights. Others laughed at me because those days, India did not have engineers by the dozen and it was the decade of the brain drain. After the announcement of the Nobel Prize, those same people who had joked about me and had never called me in 30 years, told me, "Oh Kailash, do you remember, I was in civil and you were in electrical?" (laughs). But then such is life; you have to be very focussed on and have faith in your chosen path.

Are you going to bring out a vision document, a road map or a charter of solutions with the Nobel Laureate and Leaders for Children Summit?

Well, people are fed up with theoretical discussion, papers and academic knowledge. There is a plethora of rhetoric. So, there is no use reinventing the wheel. I even have action-based solution models, but they are still awaiting practical implementation.

Despite laws and conventions, international treaties and institutions, inter-governmental organisations as well as national institutions, children are still suffering badly. This has never happened before. The world has never been so wealthy as it is today but the world has never given such pain to children ever. In terms of magnitude, there are new ways of exploiting and abusing children and denying them their rights. For example, hundreds and thousands of children are forced to lose their limbs, families and homelands and become refugees. The world's greatest humanitarian crisis is of refugee children, who are victims of multiple vulnerabilities. Few months ago, there was a shocking report that 9,000 unaccompanied minors in Germany went missing. Most of them were Syrian, some of them were from Iraq and others from North Africa. So, they entered European soil, traversed Austria, entered Germany and suddenly went missing. Similarly, about 6,000 children from Italy went missing. Interpol suspects that these children must have been trafficked by some organised crime network for slavery, prostitution or raising terrorist militia. Over the last few years, the largest number of young people have been brainwashed and many of them have become terrorists or suicide bombers. The average age is 16; boys and girls are killing themselves to kill others.

Also, children are the worst sufferers of natural disasters, which are becoming more frequent due to global warming and climate change. Many young girls, who were victims of the Nepal earthquake, were not only trafficked to Indian but European brothels as well. We found that some of these girls had been trafficked to as far as England. That's why I say children are the worst sufferers despite all this progress that we have made as a civilisation.

So, where are we lacking? In my experience, it is moral power. Right from individual rights to political, social and economic ones, collective morality is missing. That's what propelled me to think of a universal platform where moral leaders from the world could speak in one strong language that enough is enough, our children need to be protected now from violence, prejudice and exploitative systems.

Then the Nobel Peace Prize boosted my efforts for it was the first time the Peace Prize recognised the right of the child to a healthy society. Over the last two years, I got several occasions to interact with laureates of different disciplines and was able to coalesce a common dream of creating a sustainable future for our children.

How did you manage to get them together for a common cause?

I was lucky enough to meet them for different occasions, be it global warming, disaster management, and so on. I used every encounter to prioritise child issues. Wherever I went, whatever the subject of discussion, I spoke only about children. It was then that I realised that many of the science laureates, economists and litterateurs did not even know that child slavery existed in the modern world. They were shocked by figures that 168 million children were working as child labour. Out of them, five-and-a-half million, according to UN statistics, are literally slaves or bonded labour in the agricultural sector, mining, quarrying and small-scale industries. Domestic child labour is a serious problem in most fast-growing economies, including India, Brazil and South Africa. The fishing industry is another exploitative mechanism. Though South Asia and West Africa are the hub of these practices, I came across bonded child labourers in USA whom we are helping to free themselves. There are children who are trafficked from Latin American countries. Cambodia, Thailand and Philippines are known for child prostitution.

Presented with facts, most Nobel laureates expressed their willingness to take up the issue of child rights in their own way; maybe use the knowledge of their discipline too. In all our meetings, I told them that while their intellectual power had bettered human lives, from polio eradication to technology, they had eventually benefitted corporations. Their moral authority, power and outreach had not been properly harnessed for the cause of the most vulnerable section of the society — children. That was a trigger.

Similarly, I realised that a large number of world leaders like former Presidents, Prime Ministers and their wives as well as royalty were doing a lot of work, charity mostly, but nothing in the direction which could bring about systemic change in the society and in the world. I tapped into their compassion for children.

Some big economists, those who have drafted millennial and sustainable development goals, engaged in child-specific discussions and debated coordinated actionable plans, like what we can do together. It was then that I proposed this idea of a laureate and leaders' summit for children. About 34 laureates showed interest, 14 of whom are visiting India. The first edition will be in India and keep on rolling across countries along with ongoing activities born out of putting heads together.

I call it a movement, a movement for globalisation of compassion. A globalised economy is a powerful tide that has pulled everybody along. But when we talk about India, it has its own set of deep-rooted values and systems. So, let us just dig out one value and that value or virtue could be transformed into a social movement, that is compassion. Gandhiji took up seemingly simple issues like *ahimsa* (non-violence) and *satya* (truth). People then thought these were ideals best taught in temples and not tangible or workable in the real world, but he was able to build a social movement out of it. Similarly, we also have to create a worldwide social movement around compassion because it is a wealth which everybody in the world has. We are born with that. So, all we've got to do is break the shells of ego and selfishness in order to unlock our compassion and see what kind of world we make for our children.

To what extent will demonetisation in India have an impact on child trafficking?

It is a lesser known fact that human trafficking and child labour are among the largest sources of black money. I have come across innumerable incidents where the agent or middleman earned at least ₹ 5,000 for the placement of young boys as bonded labour and in cases of girls sold for prostitution and child marriages, this amount was around ₹ 2 lakh.

Every single rupee earned by the traffickers and slave masters is black money. This move will break their backbone. According to a study conducted by Global March against Child Labour, ₹ 21 lakh crore is generated by enslaving young girls in brothels. Another study conducted by 'Bachpan Bachao Andolan' reveals huge sums of money which are blatantly stolen in the name of wages paid to child labourers. Take, for instance, the government estimate of child labour in India — 43 lakh children, who are to be paid around ₹ 250 each every day. In reality though, these children will receive around ₹ 50 only. That is ₹ 200 stolen per child, per day, every day. And these are just the government figures. Non-government studies claim the black market to be much stronger.

Anything specific to India that you have worked on, which can be a solution-based model for the government, private citizens or civil society?

There is no dearth of solutions or solution-based models across the world. In some cases, the government took it up, like in Brazil some years ago, where it introduced a conditional cash transfer programme for mothers. It entailed transferring $ 80 to their bank accounts, provided they sent their children to school. This led to empowerment of the mothers on the condition that their children attend school on a regular basis. Similarly, in India, the mid-day meal programme, despite its corruption-driven faulty implementation in parts, has been largely successful. Social protection programmes, like MNREGA, have helped a lot.

I have proposed that all these programmes be coordinated in such a manner that parents can be given work only when they send their children to schools. So, children can attend schools and be weaned off from workplaces while compliant parents would be preferred for MNREGA schemes.

My own experiments relate to creating child-friendly villages, which we began in India and have replicated in Nepal, Uganda and Peru. We have about 500 child-friendly villages in India now. I started with villages because that is where children are exploited in the farm sector and allied activities and trafficked to big cities as cheap labour and helps. A child-friendly village is one where children are free from exploitation or abuses, be it child labour, child marriage, trafficking and child sexual abuse. Second, all the children must be attending schools, irrespective of caste or community. Third, all village children must form their own representative body or *bal panchayat*, a bottom-up structure to build a culture of democracy rather than a top-down approach. This instills democratic values right from their childhood. And democracy is not a system of government, it's a culture. So, children must learn that. Fourth, village *panchayats* have to recognise and work with *bal panchayats* to make policies that enable a healthy generation next.

This is such an innovative model that children not only learn, they speak and interact directly with the powers that be and argue cogently for diverting resources in their direction in a need-based manner. It was only through this experiment that we found out that 90 per cent school dropouts in villages occurred due to the absence of a separate toilet for girls and safe drinking water. This was much before the toilet-building revolution or the Swachh Bharat mission. So, we had already constructed more than 400 toilets in these villages. And for a country that is often blasted for being gender-insensitive, it was the boys who made toilets for girls a key plank of their election manifesto before they were elected to the *bal panchayat*. The other demands were for a library and ensuring the mid-day meal that did not compromise on quality and quantity. When the children themselves became their own leaders, it was impossible for policy-makers to overlook their concerns.

Do you think that our national child policies need any upgrade, amendment or recast? What needs to be done in India's context?

I have asked the Prime Minister to launch a campaign for a child-friendly India in much the same manner as the other campaigns. I would want it to be linked with the Swachh Bharat and Beti Bachao, Beti Padhao drives. It should even be linked to Make in India, making it mandatory for investors to adhere to some of the fundamental values of protecting child rights as well as ensure ethical labour practices.

Coming back to your point, the most important aspect is to prioritise children in budgetary allocations. We are all proud of being one of the youngest nations. And what is our demographic dividend? Forty per cent of our population is below the age of 14, but it is shocking that we spend only 4 per cent of the GDP for their education, health and protection. What else could be more inappropriate? Our education and health spendings show that children are not our priority.

Let us begin with investing in our future generation. And this is not about the government, but about our social will. Sure there is lack of political will but equally alarming is our social will to deal with our children impartially. We can do everything and anything for those born to us but when it comes to the mistreatment of other children, we just choose to look the other way. We don't raise a bogey, we don't stop hiring teenager maids, thinking they must be capable, considering they have attained puberty. Yet they are the most vulnerable physically.

I have also been talking to faith leaders across borders to propagate child rights as part of their core teachings. Each of our faith leaders has a huge following, is heard with seriousness and earns huge money from donations. But you will hardly find them uttering a single sentence for children. I have never heard any faith leader of merit saying that anybody who violates the dignity of a girl or child would not be considered a part of his said religion. They talk for hours but never talk about child rights or ostracising their abusers. A social worker or NGO organising an awareness camp in a village would not have as much impact as when a religious leader posits himself/herself as the protector of children. It would seem like a moral duty rather than moral bankruptcy.

Let's face it, a lot of activism in India is also under the scanner for being motivated or being funded for a specific objective. How does this affect your operations?

I think activists, NGOs and civil society organisations represent the same society as politicians and business houses do. So, there are bound to be manipulative errants. In the end, it is a matter of national character. Some of the small, unacknowledged organisations working at the grassroots are so genuine and hard-working. Husbands and wives have given up lucrative jobs and are even raising their children in remote pockets in an attempt to mainstream India's future generations. People are working ceaselessly to change society and it would be unfair to generalise their efforts. In fact, genuine efforts may get swamped but are the reason that I go on.

Looking at the larger picture, I would say that both in India and the world, the State was largely looked up to as the protector of human rights and development about 20 years ago. The State was expected to execute and implement schemes and allocate funds for them. We, the civil society, were fighting for a space at UN meetings to deliberate on child rights, poverty alleviation, ecological issues and global warming. That discourse has changed. The change is evident when you compare the charters for millennium development and sustainable development goals. In the first, civil society was sitting on the fringes, giving inputs to government and inter-governmental agencies. It deepened and broadened in the latter. Then the corporates came in, not directly but indirectly through the World Economic Forum. The Director-General of WEF was part of a high-level group on education.

Today, for any institutional mechanism and flagship programme, we have strong representation of the civil society and corporates beside the state and inter-governmental organisations. Human rights were supposed to be a very exclusive portfolio of the government because they had to deal with the laws and Constitution, and so on. But now the corporates and civil societies are being counted in. Hence, a tussle of perception ensues.

Don't you think too much of corporate involvement could cause tweaking of priorities from the development perspective?

The meaning of corporate social responsibility or CSR has been so narrowed down that it's normally perceived as some philanthropic activity and utilising 2 per cent of your budget. Some countries have no CSR mandate at all. CSR cannot be seen as a transference of guilt. We cannot exploit resources, water and people in the geographical area of our operation and set up schools and charitable projects elsewhere. True CSR is when we respect the people and planet where our operations are.

Have more corporates come to you after your Nobel win?

As a matter of fact, there are fewer corporates for our initiatives. Most of them invest their money in flagship programmes run by the government. Some of them even put a large amount of money in some of the very conventional efforts for children's education.

Finally, what are the challenges that need urgent redress in the context of children in India?

First of all, we should listen to our children, really listen to them. There should be a whole paradigm shift in our mindset. We keep imposing our ambitions, thinking and goals on them. Instead, we should acknowledge their purity, simplicity and transparency. We should establish a different kind of relationship with our children which is beyond adoring and simply loving them. It should be a bond of friendship. Second, we should educate them not for the sake of material sustenance, but to strengthen human values and culture. Third, we have to create institutions, mechanisms and a culture of accountability. Fourth, we need an independent body for child welfare. The existing institutions come under various ministries. So, they don't have the moral authority because they themselves are accountable for their work to the ministers or bureaucrats and not to the children. The fourth challenge is budget re-allocation. We have to prioritise our children's education, healthcare and protection.

Lastly, we should have a more holistic approach. There is so much fragmentation between and among departments dealing with one child issue. We should have more coordinated inter-departmental or inter-ministerial segments on the policy level as well as practice modules.

The most imminent danger is from cyber space, which is being manipulated and misused to a large extent. School-going kids fall into mischief-makers' trap very easily. Girls are exploited to an extent where they even contemplate suicide. And the social taboo is so deep-rooted that children don't even share these things at their home with their elders. These are some of the very serious problems which children have never faced before. And the less privileged ones have a greater chance of being victimised. So, this is why we are going to come out with a strong moral call.

❑

5
Every Child Matters

Winner of the Nobel Peace Prize in 2014 and identified globally as one of the most influential child-rights activists, Kailash Satyarthi speaks to Preeti Singh about his switch from being an engineer to a full-time social worker in the 1980s, his ongoing national and international projects, and the need to push for comprehensive social reforms if we are to eradicate the evil of exploitative child labour.

In the 80s, you gave up your engineering career and began campaigning against child labour and for child rights. You also founded the 'Bachpan Bachao Andolan' at this time. So, what impelled you to make such a radical career move and become a social activist?

Well, the influence of marginalised children was very close to my heart from my own childhood and my concern grew up gradually. So, that was a kind of an inner calling when I realised that I am not going to do justice with my passion. And I decided to give up my career. It was not just one single incident, but was a gradual growth of this concern. Like every family, my parents also had some expectations and aspirations from me and when they found that I was good in studies, they wanted me to become an engineer. So, I was enrolled in an engineering college and I passed out from there and started teaching in a university.

I trace back the roots of my concern, though, to my own childhood. It was my first day at school. I was five-and-a-half years old and I saw a cobbler boy sitting outside my school gate. And he was looking at us expectantly, hoping we'll ask him to polish our shoes, but we all were wearing new shoes. And I could not understand why this child was not a part of our classroom like other children. So, I asked my teacher; asked my family and friends — and most of them tried to convince me that it is not an uncommon practice as poor children have to work to help their families, and so on. One day, I gathered some courage and directly spoke to the father of the boy. The boy was of my age. The father was shocked at this question and he said, *"Babuji, maine kabhi socha nahi* [Sir, I have never thought about it]. My grandfather, then my father and I started doing the same thing since childhood and now my son." Then he said, *"Babuji, aapko pata nahin hum karam karne ke liye hi paida huye hain*! [Sir, don't you know we're born only to work]." So, there was hopelessness and helplessness, both. It was difficult for me to understand this. But I was angry that people are saying something else and for this cobbler, he and his son are non-existent in society and are born to work. In later years, I tried to collect money to help poor children and collected books from schools for them, and it went on, until one day, I decided to go for it full-time.

How do you identify areas or sectors where exploitative child labour might be rampant?

We know that most of these children work in unorganised sector. Sixty per cent of the children work in the agricultural sector alone, and the rest of them work in sectors like brick kilns, stone-quarries, small-scale industries in urban setups; then as domestic child labour and on streets, working in *dhabas,* and some are thrown into prostitution. Some are in carpet-making bangle-making and so on. These are the areas. Normally, parents who complain to us are those whose children are kidnapped or lured away on the basis of some false promise. And the children are not caring enough or sending any money back home. So, it's through parents or relatives that we come to know about such areas.

Do you think education is enough to curb child labour and what kind of change do we need in our education system to be able to solve this problem?

Not really. Although education is really important, perhaps most important is to take preventive measures. If children are enrolled in schools and receive good-quality education or free education and are in child-friendly environments, then a large number of them would not enter the job market. So, education is the key. If every village has good education for children, then there are less chances of child-trafficking. Similarly, children who withdraw from child labour ought to be inducted in mainstream education. And those who are grown-ups, they should be given some special training. But there is a vicious circle between child labour, unemployment and illiteracy. Globally, 70 crore children are in full-time jobs and 21 crore adults are jobless. Most of these adults are the very parents of these children who are child labourers. Children are preferred because they are cheap labourers and parents remain jobless. That is the vicious circle. Parents remain poor and poverty pushes children to work and if the children are working, poverty would increase and they remain poor. So, the third dimension is education. Education is the key to empowerment, social justice and gender equality. But definitely there are other things that are needed. We need strong political will, strong laws and accountability on the part of the officers who are responsible for the enforcement of child labour laws. We need strong corporate social responsibilities and very strong commitment of the corporations that no child will be engaged in their supply chains. Only a combination of these things will help.

But there are children who are enrolled in government schools and work as domestic helps after school gets over. How can our government schools tackle the challenge of curbing child labour?

Actually, education should promote empowerment, human values and humanity. It should also produce a more equitable society. There are children who are enrolled in government schools and work in the afternoons, but that is not applicable to expensive private schools as private school education is qualitatively better, though expensive. So, our education system creates a duality, a disparity in society. We have to ensure that our government schools are improved — so that boys and girls and can learn at these institutions and stay interested enough to continue their schooling. We need well-educated teachers who have some sense of accountability towards their students. Similarly, we need to think of how some vocational training can be given to children between the ages of 15 and 18. Some light skills can be indroduced in the curriculum, so that when the kids turn 18, they can earn a livelihood. Any vocational training which doesn't lumper their health can be introduced. But this should not start before the completion of their secondary education.

I have been working in 140 countries in the last 30 years to eradicate the problem of child labour, but now my agenda has gone to its highest level. Now I am able to share Internet with high officials and I get respect, thanks to the Nobel Prize. The man is the same but this award has made all the difference.

Money troubles often force families to sell their children into servitude. According to you, what steps can be taken to protect children from being exploited in this way?

To being with social protection programmes should be properly enforced. There are several programmes, like MGNREGA, scholarships for children, incentives for children as well as for women and men below the poverty line, lower castes, Scheduled Castes and Scheduled Tribes. So, these government schemes should be properly enforced. That will help. And, in some cases, economic incentive programmes are not known to parents and children. These incentives should be offered to those who need them.

In July this year, a controversial law was passed that would allow children to work for family businesses, despite widespread concern by the United Nations and other rights advocates that it will push more children into exploitative labour. What is your take on that?

I was part of all these discussions and I opposed it, but I have not given up. I am still in contact with the ministers to accommodate some rules. There are certain areas which could be included in these rules, like a list of hazardous occupations and processes. Earlier, the list included 83 hazardous occupations in the previous norm; now it has been reduced to three. The government is considering taking it back. We, too, are working on it and we are hopeful that things of our concern would be addressed.

What about the children who are working in the entertainment sector, who are pushed by their parents to appear on reality shows and so on? How do you view this trend?

There are laws like Juvenile Justice Act which make it very difficult for these people to use children as a workforce to earn more money through them within the entertainment industry. So, these things are now being taken care of, but it requires a lot of social awareness as well because parents can also be quite greedy at times. Many are promoting their children to join TV shows and to taste some glamour through them. Everyone wants a glamorous life and these parents want to be the parents of celebrity children. This often impacts children's education and interferes with their free time and can hamper their physical and mental health. If the children are learning and expressing their talent through such forums, then that's an altogether different issue. But if the parents have some motive of earning through their children at the cost of their mental and physical health, then that is wrong. There is a very thin line here. That is why, I said it's very necessary that the parents themselves should be aware of these things and should know when they're crossing the line.

What are the major campaigns that you are working on now?

Now we are working on two major things — one is a campaign and the other is a big initiative. We are going to launch a platform of Nobel laureates and global leaders. The laureates and leaders for children's summit will concentrate on building a strong moral platform for protecting children from violence and ensuring a world where all children are free to be children. This summit will amplify the collective leadership and moral authority of Nobel laureates across different fields, world leaders and champions of children's rights. (The summit was held in Delhi from 10 to 11 December.) Then we have another activity — we are lunching a campaign called '100 Million for a 100 Million'. It's a youth campaign where the school-going and college-going young people are able to express themselves, learn about their rights and feel responsible towards the 100 million kids who are tortured, who have no childhood, no education. So, these 100 million children with a better life can be the spokespersons and chain-persons for the cause of the 100 million who are left out.

Do you think the National Commission for Protection of Child Rights is doing enough for underprivileged children?

I think they are much better than before. There was a kind of dormant situation for many years, but now, they are gearing up towards initiatives and activities and I appreciate that. First of all, they have members in the Commission. For many years, there was no member in the Commission; the Commission was completely vacant. Even a chairman was not appointed. Now there is a chairperson and the members are allocated responsibility in child labour, education, child abuse. They are now taking care of it. And they are quite dynamic. I met a few of themselves and found that they are travelling around; they are also associating with the government and other agencies and working closely with the civil society; and they are working hard, including the chairperson.

How has your journey been after receiving the Nobel Peace Prize in 2014 for your work on child rights?

The journey is now more hectic. I have been working with 140 countries in about 30 years to eradicate this problem, but now my agenda has gone to its highest level. Now I am able to interact with high officials and people more freely and I get respect, thanks to this Nobel Prize. The man is the same but this award made all the difference.

Have you ever been subjected to personal threats due to the kind of work you do? And what keeps you going?

Several times! I lost two of my colleagues — one was shot and one was beaten to death. My office and my house have been attacked. Once my office was put on fire and I had my left foot broken and my right shoulder broken. I still can't move my shoulder properly and this happened some years ago. The attacks have prevailed for the last three decades. These people are mafia gangs who are into trafficking children. I have helped free more than 85,000 children so far. This keeps inspiring me. One life is not enough to protect these thousands of children.

❑

6
We don't have Adequate Political Will

In a first of Straight Talk series, the reporters of The Asian Age *interacted with Nobel laureate Kailash Satyarthi to discuss child labour in the country, whether the Nobel Prize has helped change the outlook towards child exploitation and how effective is the Child Labour Bill, which was recently passed in the Parliament.*

Sanjay Basak: Tell us about your journey as a relentless crusader of child rights. What do you think about the present child labour law?

I started my fight against child labour in India when India didn't have any specific law on child labour. So, it's a long journey. In 1981, when we started our mission, there was some mention of child labour in old British laws, but we didn't have any specifics. It was not just about the law but nobody was talking about slavery, child labour. Trafficking is a new phrase that came into existence 10 years ago. So, we had to fight for a law in India. I recall those days when we demonstrated in front of Parliament, but the law that was enacted was a very poor and weak law. It justified under the garb of regulation most of the child work. We were never satisfied with that law. But apart from this, the biggest shame was that the law was never properly implemented. Later on, we had other laws, like Right to Education (RTE) and the Juvenile Justice (JJ) Act. So, all the children had to be protected up to the age of 18 years. We had a strong reason to claim and demand that India should have a law, which can sink with the two progressing laws.

We have been demanding it since the last government. We had series of discussions with the previous government and this government for a comprehensive and strong law, under which all forms of child labour is prohibited up to the age of 14 and all forms of hazardous activities are prohibited up to the age of 18 years. There were two fundamental things. But now, unfortunately, we have two major lacunae. One is that it blurs the line between family work or learning in the family and exploitation by the so-called family members. The present law allows the work of all children in family enterprises and the family's definition is too long. The second serious problem is the prohibited part of the law. Earlier, 83 occupations and processes were prohibited for children's work because they were hazardous. Now it has been slashed to three. The children could be allowed to work in brick kilns, slaughter-houses, *bidi*-making, rolling. So, these are the serious problems. The law didn't touch the rehabilitation part.

Sanjay Basak: Child labour is a major problem but then there is the poverty factor. They can't even eat properly and that's one of the reasons that children are put to work. This is a social problem in a way.

It's a social evil and it's a crime. Globally speaking, there are studies in India, Peru, Nigeria, Philippines, Pakistan, Mexico and several countries where it has been established that there is a parallel between the parents' unemployment and the children's employment. There was a study that proved that if parents are not able to find jobs for more than 100 days a year, then their children can go to work. If children are employed, they are preferred as the cheapest source of labour or free labour sometimes, if they are bonded labour. They cannot form unions, they can't go to a court of law and they can't change all the atrocities they have to face. So, the children are always physically and mentally vulnerable to exploitation, and the parents remain jobless.

The second thing is that we have almost 200 million children up to the age of 18 and are supposed to be in schools but they are not in schools. Sixty million children have never been to schools and 140 million children are school dropouts. So, it is also linked with education. I have been propagating/advocating a triangular paradigm relationship: child labour, poverty and illiteracy; they have cause-and-consequence relationship or chicken-and-egg relationship. If you allow child labour, then the parents adults will remain unemployed and the poverty will continue. But, on the other hand, children will be deprived of schooling.

The present law allows the work of all children in family enterprises and the family's definition is too long. The second problem is the prohibited part of the law. Earlier, 83 occupations were prohibited for children's work because they were hazardous; now it has been slashed to three.

Manish Anand: We have been on the new path of globalisation and the country has progressed economically quite fast. So, have you seen data that suggests that economic development can really address or the number has gone down for the children involved in child labour?

No, actually, it has helped, indirectly also. The schemes like MNREGA, the mid-day meal scheme and so many other social protection programmes have helped in the decrease of child labour. The trend is definitely clear that the number of child labourers is declining. But what is visible now is trafficking. There are girls trafficked from Assam and married in Haryana.

Rajnish Sharma: Has the conviction rate improved?

Not significantly. So has been the case with POSCO — only 0.6 per cent convictions have been made. That has not been implemented effectively.

Teena Thacker: Since you have said that you are not satisfied with the child labour law, the amendments, what is your next plan of action? Are you going to meet the PM on this?

I made my point clear to the Prime Minister, and several times to the Minister of Labour. And I am not just blaming the government, but the Opposition is equally responsible because they could have halted it in the Rajya Sabha. I have met almost every single top opposition leader this time and the government before.

Sanjay Basak: Do you see lack of political will?

We definitely don't have adequate political will. We still see our children with a commercial or economic or income-generation lens, not with a moral or humanitarian one.

Sanjay Basak: Do you also see lack of awareness among politicians?

Of course, you can see the level of debate in the Rajya Sabha and then in the Lok Sabha. The good thing is that there were many people who spoke strongly against this law. That happened for the first time, but most of the people who spoke were not aware of the consequences of these lacunae. Or they didn't speak with the passion that was needed.

Rajnish Sharma: Do you have a rough estimate on children being illegally trafficked from India?

Nobody has an idea. Actually, there are new trafficking hubs emerging. Earlier, traditionally children were trafficked from Chhattisgarh, Odisha and some parts of Bihar to work as domestic help, as well as to work as child forced labour. Some of them were also trafficked for child prostitution. They were from Nepal and West Bengal normally. Now the north-eastern region has become one of the biggest-trafficking hubs — from Assam, also from Arunachal Pradesh and adjoining parts of West Bengal, several districts have emerged as trafficking hubs. And these girls — girls and boys both — specially girls are trafficked for everything and anything, right? From child bride to child prostitution to child labour, and so on. The boys are trafficked from Assam to work in Tamil Nadu and Karnataka. We have rescued children from Bengaluru as they were trafficked from Assam. The human trafficking business was a $ 45 billion industry just five-six years ago. And the latest figures reveal that it has become a 150-billion-dollar industry.

Rajnish Sharma: How much is the figure for India?

Unfortunately, India is a destination. So, children are trafficked from Nepal and Bangladesh basically to work in India. India is a source. Children are trafficked to other places from India.

Manish Anand: We have been clamouring for laws for any kind of social abuse, we demand that laws be passed. In Delhi, begging is a crime. There is a law against it, but at every roundabout, you see children as beggars. So, when laws are not enforced, what is the meaning of laws?

I have been fighting for laws and I have been successful in some ways, but only laws can't change society. I can't see any history where laws have transformed society. Laws can help, but they can't be the only way to transform society. Social consciousness is very important. We have to build consciousness in society. And that is why, I have been appealing to faith leaders of different communities to speak strongly for children. But you hardly see this.

Sanjay Basak: How many gurus, *sadhus* and saints speak on this? You must have met Baba Ramdev? What kind of response are you getting?

No, I never met Baba Ramdev. I have been writing to them for many, many years. They don't answer all these questions. I also met the Pope and he keeps on speaking about social issues, but we need much more strong voices from the faith leaders and right from the bottom. I have been talking to some Muslim leaders, also the other leaders.

Suparna Sharma: As you said, child labour is a social evil. Does it help when the PM of the country romanticises his own days as a child labourer — a *chaiwala*?

It's true that he was a *chaiwala.* I have appealed to him that he has gone through suffering, mental trauma of selling tea on the railway platform and now he is a powerful PM and it is his turn to ensure that no child is compelled to become a child labourer or a *chaiwala* and I hope that he will be working on it.

Suparna Sharma: But sending out this message repeatedly, does that help?

I don't know but many people think if a *chaiwala* can become the PM, why can't they too? It may be helping in creating more hope in the minds of the youngsters or poor people.

That's one part of it but now he has to make sure that no child is bound to sell tea on the platform in the street of any form of child labour.

Yojna Gusai: Are you happy with the way NCPCR is working?

NCPCR is gearing up. It was defunct; there was no chairperson and members for quite some time.

Suparna Sharma: Once you have rescued children from any situation, have you seen them come back?

We saw that before, but that is negligible now and I have learnt this from my own experience.

Once we rescue, we make sure that they are rescued under appropriate law. So, it is not simply by going and liberating them with the help of police.

We used to liberate the children under the bonded labour law or juvenile justice, then the Minimum Age Act, Contract Labour Act. We try to bring every possible law in picture and then try to act accordingly so that these children who are freed are entitled to rehabilitation.

You can see the level of debate in Rajya Sabha and then in the Lok Sabha. The good thing is that there were many people who spoke strongly against this law. That happened for the first time. But most of the people who spoke were not aware of the consequences of these lacunae.

❑

7

Child Trafficking Accounts for a Good Chunk of Black Money

It is a sleepy afternoon outside Kailash Satyarthi's Kalkaji residence, but the flurry of activities inside belie the quietude outside. Calls have just come in from Mumbai about a dozen children being left alone at a railway station and the Nobel laureate's phone keeps ringing.

Satyarthi is launching an initiative that will bring in global leaders to speak out against violence against children. He is bringing 14 Nobel laureates to the capital for the project – Leaders and Laureates – on December 10th and 11th this year. He will also launch a youth-for-youth programme — 100 million for 100 million — which will mobilise 100 million well-to-do young people to help another 100 million in need.

"If a government in any country makes laws which are regressive to children, or cuts budgetary allocation earmarked for children, or if the overseas development budget is not up to the promises made globally, we will raise those issues," says Satyarthi.

Ahead of Children's Day on Monday (today), Satyarthi spoke to DNA about his initiative, about the lack of will among our political class to fight for children and about mobilising the young to bring changes.

Excerpts:

You have spoken out against child laws that are regressive. In India, the Child Labour Act, which was

amended this year, has invited a lot of flak. Similarly, the Trafficking of Persons (Prevention, Protection and Rehabilitation) Bill, currently in discussion, has been derided on several counts.

Think for a while, think about the power that about 100 million young people will wield. Of course, not everyone will join at one go, but several million will be on board initially. And, when this moral platform of global leaders gets working, as the youth protest and appeal to their governments, pieces of legislation, like the Child Labour Amendment Bill, will not pass. The Bill has passed now, but several concerns plague almost all countries. It is our moral duty to stop that.

This was one of the reasons that motivated me to think in that direction. Creating a safer world for children; it is not an idealism. I think it is equally important to influence political will through moral power, which is something lacking in the world today.

As far as the Trafficking Bill is concerned, we have been working on it at the 'Bachpan Bachao Andolan'. We are in close touch with the authorities and hope that this will be a good Bill. We have seen some progressive elements, like in the case of the Juvenile Justice Act, when we helped the government draft the model draft rules.

You have said many times that black money and trafficking share a deep relationship. Do you think demonetisation will help?

I know that the common man is facing a lot of difficulties with the demonetisation drive in several ways. But I will say that the drive will definitely help curb trafficking. It will create a lot of problems for the traffickers, the slave masters and those employing child labourers.

I have spoken on black money with the previous government and the current one. When they talk of black money, the focus is on tax evasion. We have done some scientific studies and we found that human trafficking, particularly child trafficking, prostitution and child labour, account for the largest segment of black money — much more than what the government estimates. Our estimate is that the trafficking trade in India is worth ₹ 21 lakh crore, which includes the black money embedded in it.

Every single rupee generated out of a child labourer, whether it is because of the denial of daily wage, or the denial of contract labour, or the violation of child labour laws, trafficking laws and the like, becomes black money. When a girl is trafficked from Assam, usually for ₹ 10,000-₹ 15,000, and brought to Delhi or Haryana to be sold as a child bride, ₹ 1,00,000-₹ 1,50,000 change hands. If she has been brought in by placement agencies for domestic labour, she is sold for ₹ 40,000-₹ 50,000. All of this is black money.

The government, while replying to a Lok Sabha question a few years ago, accepted that a child labourer earns ₹ 20-25 a day, which means an employer spends ₹ 20-25 on him or her every day. The floor wages of an adult labourer is ₹ 120, even though the minimum wage across states is between ₹ 175 and ₹ 350.

The situation today has changed slightly. A child labourer earns around ₹ 40 and an adult around ₹ 240. An employer saves ₹ 200 on every child he or she employs. They cannot show on paper that they are employing child labourers. So, they write in wage books that they are paying ₹ 240, while they pay only ₹ 40. This is black money. For every child, the employer is saving ₹ 200 every day. If somebody is employing 50 children in a small workshop, that's ₹ 3,00,000 every month.

The good outcome of demonetisation is that it has hurt traffickers badly. Yet, in the long run, we need proper enforcement laws relating to the poor, especially those relating to children, otherwise, the situation will not change. The money will remain; only the bank notes will change.

The amendment to the Child Labour Act formalised the need for young children to earn. How does that pan out when we talk of black money in the trafficking trade?

I spoke against the Bill till the last moment. There was nothing substantial in the Lok Sabha debate. The government did not have any strong point to support the amendment and the Opposition's questions were not stinging enough.

For example, I could not gather from the discussion as to the need for child labour when there is such a large number of unemployed youth, adults and the elderly in the country. I have been pushing this argument for sometime now — globally, 170 million children are doing full-time jobs when 197 million adults are jobless. Most of the jobless are the very parents or elders who send children to work.

Children are preferred in labour-intensive industries as they are cheap, easy prey for tax evasion and cannot speak on their behalf. Adults, on the other hand, demand more money and better living conditions.

The government should have given employment schemes to parents instead. Most importantly, if the government's thought process is guided by the principles of disparity, discrimination and exclusion, children will continue to suffer. On the one hand, you are creating a club of elite young people whose aspirations touch the sky and on the other, you are telling children in villages that our country is poor. Did these children create poverty? They are already suffering from poverty and you tell them that this is the harsh reality. Why should children suffer? Educate them. The global economy owes everything to knowledge, information and technology. We are taking that away from the child in the village and asking him to drop out of school and help elders at home. That's because of the government's mental state of complacency. There's also a fair amount of vested interest.

Do you think that the Parliament lacks healthy voices to highlight social sector failures?

There are a lot of social workers in the Parliament. If we look closely, social work is also, in the long run, a form of politics. Social workers may not actively pursue politics, but they are influencing the lives of people and that's what politics is all about.

Never in the history of India had a single day been devoted to child-related issues by the Parliament. Children may not be voters, but they are our future.

That's my appeal to the government and political parties today, on Children's Day. No party has ever demanded that in the 69 years of the country's parliamentary history. Every year, for dozens of days, the Parliament does not function or business hours are wasted on frivolous issues. There has never been a demand by the parliamentarians to bring down the exploitation of girls even in the capital. They will slur or fight, but not for children. Neither inside nor outside the Parliament has it ever happened that leaders of national or regional parties have got together to discuss children's education, budgetary allocation and laws. This shows a serious lack of political will among the political class. Prioritise children in your political decisions, in policies and their implementation. If we design schemes with children in mind, a whole generation will benefit. But if we will look only at votes, benefits will percolate only for the coming five years. Accountability in the polity, society and other spheres is lacking.

In the last few decades that you have been working for children in India, where do you think is the problem most prevalent?

As far as child trafficking and child labour are concerned, the source areas have always been the eastern parts of the country — Assam, West Bengal, Bihar and Odisha. The metros, Mumbai, Delhi, Hyderabad, etc., make up for most of the destinations. These are the places which exploit children behind closed doors. Ten days ago, we carried out a big rescue operation and saved 45 children from a workshop in Delhi. We had to break this huge lock on an iron door and it was complicated and messy. Some of us went in with the police. A lot of children were hidden inside and many were sent to the terrace. They were hidden under gunny sacks and they looked terrified.

❑

8

'We Need a National Tribunal for Children'

Child rights activist Kailash Satyarthi urges President to set up the National Children's Tribunal for time-bound disposal of cases of crimes against kids.

Nobel laureate and child rights activist Kailash Satyarthi reached Delhi after completing his 11,000-km-long Bharat Yatra across 22 states, from Kashmir to Kanyakumari, against child sexual abuse.

Speaking to Soumya Pillai of *The Hindu*, Mr Satyarthi, said his Yatra was aimed at providing a platform to several children, youth and their families to speak out about the sexual abuse and violence they faced and how it scarred them.

After touring almost 22 states, you met President Ram Nath Kovind today (Monday). What were the core issues that you discussed with him?

A major issue that I experienced through my work in all these years and from the places I visited as part of the Bharat Yatra is that children in India are suffocating because of the diktat we feed to them in the garb of family, honour and dignity. They want to speak, but there is no outlet.

I have requested the President to order the creation of the National Children's Tribunal, an exclusive court to address crimes against children, in order to ensure time-bound disposal of cases. Senior judges should be part of this tribunal.

In most states, the pendency of such cases is almost 90 per cent to 95 per cent. There should also be child-friendly police stations where training should be given to police officers to handle these cases more sensitively.

What was your experience during the Bharat Yatra?

There is a major conflict between children's aspirations to grow and the social taboos they face. In most cases of abuse, children are taught to remain silent and not report the case because of family honour and the stigma attached to such crimes. Many children came running to hug me and shake hands with me during the Yatra and thanked me for providing a platform to them to speak up about their traumatic experiences.

My aim was that children and youth should break free from the stigma which is caused by a sick mentality of the society. It is this stigma which gives rise to victimisation, where children, especially girls, are made to feel vulnerable. The victims have no reason to feel guilty.

There is mass apathy from the society and this fans fear among victims and their families. Somebody had to challenge it. Change is knocking on the door. It is time that the politicians, police and the judiciary listen to it and awaken.

Were the incidents of child abuse different in different states?

There were some issues particular to some states. For example, in sensitive regions, such as Srinagar, Odisha, Madhya Pradesh and Chhattisgarh, there were cases of violence against children. In Punjab, on the other hand, many children were pushed towards drugs from an early age. We tried to address these issues, while keeping a broader umbrella of violence and abuse.

Was this Yatra just an initiative to provide a platform to these people, or were the issues taken up with the authorities?

We took up the issues of the public with the government. We also tried to involve religious leaders on the same platform so that the problem of abuse could be addressed head on.

Over 40 lakh people came forward to take a pledge to show zero tolerance towards cases of sexual abuse. Apart from this, religious leaders were made to admit that cases of abuse happen and they should denounce those who abuse children.

In many states, Chief Ministers came forward and addressed the issue of violence against children. In Kashmir, Madhya Pradesh and Punjab, the CMs assured that laws will be framed for stricter punishment for the culprits.

❑

9

'Bharat Yatra is Against a Moral Epidemic'

In an exclusive interview to India Education Diary, Nobel Prize winner Kailash Satyarthi reveals how he is taking forward his mass movement against child sexual abuse.

Why are you doing the Bharat Yatra?

Bharat Yatra is my war to end all forms of abuse. Child rape and sexual abuse have become a moral epidemic that haunts our nation. We can no longer remain silent spectators. Our silence is breeding more violence. That is why the Bharat Yatra is the beginning of an all-out war on rape, abuse and trafficking. We, at this moment, declare that we refuse to let victims and their families live in fear while the rapists roam free and fearless. I refuse to accept that eight children go missing and two are raped every hour. If a single child is in danger, India is in danger. Bharat Yatra is to make India safe again for our children. Make no mistake — this will be a decisive war; a war to reclaim the morality of the Indian soul.

Tell us about Bharat Yatra.

The Bharat Yatra is a pan-India movement to raise mass awareness about the growing menace of child sexual abuse and child trafficking. It will cover 22 States and Union Territories, spanning 11,000 kms. Moreover, I will fight for the cause of millions of children, for their safety, security and freedom. The Bharat Yatra will be organised between September to October 2017, from Kanyakumari to Delhi with smaller Yatras culminating in Delhi from all other zones of the country. Through the Yatra, the aim is to ensure that the topic of child sexual abuse and assault becomes a subject of conversation in every household, at every level. It aims to create a conversation so powerful that it will force stakeholders and visionaries across the country to relook and re-work the methods of prevention of violence against children and the redressal available to them.

When and how did the idea trigger you?

I have advocated for the safety and security of the children across the world, for over 35 years and have launched marches that have led to the inclusion of education as a fundamental right and the ratification of the ILO conventions.

The Bharat Yatra conceptualised on the theme of *'Surakshit Bachpan, Surakshit Bharat'* (Safe Childhood, Safe India) is the movement of the 21st century which will combat the evils of all forms of violence against children.

I will not let the parents of these children live in pain, helplessness, trauma and shame for the rest of their lives. Children are the future of India and there should be no place for child rapists in the country.

What is the whole motive of Bharat Yatra?

It is critical to make the public aware of the extent and seriousness of the crimes of trafficking and sexual abuse. Public mobilisation and mass awareness creation help in bringing this issue to the centre stage for social awakening and action. The Yatra will look to change the mindset of the people and sensitise them to the most urgent and pressing issue of child sexual abuse and child trafficking. How this abuse is, in fact, an organised crime?

It will become the 'voice' of the children, unable to speak up and fight for their dignity. By exploiting children through labour, sex and torture, people only lay the foundation for social, political and economic destruction of our country. This march pushes for the specificity that a Bill tabled in the Parliament will provide. If passed, the Bill will finally define the ambiguity surrounding the action necessary to be taken in cases of child trafficking.

How many participants are you expecting in this Yatra?

As this Yatra will look to involve the people in this country to fight for their future, people from all walks of life will join us. By the end of this Yatra, we aim to have at least one crore Indians join us and take a pledge to fight against child sexual abuse and trafficking. My Foundation and I have been in talks with several faith leaders, parliamentarians, corporates, etc., all of whom have whole-heartedly declared support for the Yatra and have promised that their supporters and employees would also join us to Make India Safe Again for our children.

❑

10
We have a Long Way to Go

Nobel laureate Kailash Satyarthi cannot stop lamenting about the lack of enforcement agencies working together towards eradicating a social evil. Speaking to Lakshmy Venkateswaran of The New Indian Express, *about the 'woefully inadequate' amendments to the law on child labour, he calls for a system of education that's based on equality, inclusivity, quality and lifelong learning.*

Your fight against child labour — how successful has it been?

When I began working on the issue in 1981, child labour was a non-issue. There was no law anywhere in the world, including India, and the media showed no interest in it either. People had various reasons to employ children and the most common was that poor kids needed money and that they were earning it. After we organised the Global March Against Child Labour in 1998 (unprecedented 80,000 kms across 103 countries), there was a public outcry for an international legislation to combat the worst forms of child labour, like slavery, trafficking and also using them as soldiers. Several laws were enacted and the ILO convention against the worst forms of child labour followed because of it. From 260 million children employed in labour in 1999-2000 globally, it fell to 168 million in the last 15 years. Have I eradicated child labour entirely? No! It's a long battle but we have had some victories (smiles).

Okay, now we have a law, which was even recently amended, and it...

(Interrupts) It is woefully inadequate! The amendment is not good at all. It allows children under 14 to work in their family-run businesses and the number of hazardous occupations has been reduced from 83 to three (glass furnaces, *bidi*-making, brick kilns and *zari* factories). I have rescued so many children from their extended families who were using these kids like slaves. How can children be safe anywhere if they are used for labour?

Many families encourage their kids to stop studying because they have family-owned businesses. How do you convince them this is wrong?

In 'Bachpan Bachchao Andolan', we have this concept called *Bal Mitr Gaon*, which is being followed by hundreds of villages. All children are withdrawn from child labour and rescued from child marriages; all children are made to attend school, and those who go to school form a Children's Parliament (*bal panchayat*) and the village *panchayats* agree to work with them. We also have former bonded labourers who are now employed for a monthly salary. They speak up in front of these *panchayats* and also families. For instance, when a woman inspector speaks at schools and events — it's a big deal in villages when a child enters the police force — she becomes a role model for families. We have the *Mukthi Caravan*, a campaign on wheels, where many former child labourers, now trained in theatre and story-telling, speak to the public about child rights.

Speaking of Children's Parliament, why is there no representation to kids with disabilities?

First of all, the government has to ensure that schools have all the facilities for children with disabilities — bathrooms, classrooms, black-boards, staircases, etc. If the environment in which they live is inaccessible, how can they represent anyone? Make accessibility a part of social equality.

Where are disabled children employed?

Most rescued kids with disabilities are found on the streets, begging, or in agriculture, and those without legs are found in weaving units and the embroidery sector.

How can violators be held accountable?

Accountability by enforcement agencies is missing in all laws relating to children, except for POCSO. There are too many parallel bodies involved in enforcement. Child Labour Act, Juvenile Justice Act, POCSO, education, health, etc. don't work together. They have to be inter-linked. When there is so much fragmentation and compartmentalisation of policy, it doesn't leave much room for effective solutions. Efforts to combat any social evil should be more collaborative and coordinated. Education being the fundamental right of a child is a great start but if other factors prevent a child's learning, then how can you eradicate or prevent children from the streets?

There's a school of thought that believes that vocational or skill-based learning is more useful for children than basic school education. Comment.

India's commitment to sustainable development depends on a system of education that has four components: inclusion, quality, equity and lifelong learning. Even if one is compromised, the system fails. I'm not against vocational training at all, but why apply it only to a certain section of society? Why not link both basic education and skill-based training? If we restrict the latter to just poor people, we are widening the socio-economic chasm, propagating social disparity and reinforcing caste hierarchy.

Children living on the streets have survival skills that cannot be taught in a classroom. When you rescue street children, how do you integrate them into the school system?

First, a lot of money is needed! The new Juvenile Justice Act has a strong component of children needing care and protection. This requires investment or budget allocation by the Central and State Governments. The money allocated for the welfare and rehabilitation of rescued children is miserably low. Second, people must understand that children rescued from bonded labour, streets, trafficking, etc. suffer a lot of trauma. They're used and abused to the extent that they don't trust anyone. We have to earn their trust and we cannot do it immediately.

How do you 'earn their trust'?

For instance, in the *ashrams* that my wife and I run in Delhi and Rajasthan, rescued children are given two to three weeks to get used to an abuse-free environment. This is done to restore a sense of freedom, dignity and self-esteem. Let them know that it's their choice. They don't know what to do — they're shy, timid and often scared. Many are not used to sitting on chairs; they have been victims of the worst sort of discrimination we can think of. They're used to working all the time like slaves. So, they don't understand why it's okay for them not to work but just eat and sleep whenever they want to. Kids addicted to drugs and also rescued from trafficking, take more time and need more help before they open up. We have counsellors and psychiatrists to help them.

❑

11

'All Children are Our Children'

The man who fought to make child labour a crime against humanity came to Washington, D.C. last week with a message for America and its new President.

Kailash Satyarthi, who won the Nobel Peace Prize in 2014 for his efforts to end child labour, urged U.S. lawmakers to fight for the freedom of 168 million children forced to work due to poverty, trafficking or slavery.

Those in power have a duty to "protect and care for our young people," says the 63-year-old founder of the Kailash Satyarthi Children's Foundation.

A former engineer, who turned to activism decades ago, Satyarthi successfully convinced the International Labour Organisation to prohibit child labour in 1999. We spoke to him about whether employing children can ever be justified, a new Bollywood movie in which he's a character and what advice he has for America's new President.

This interview has been edited for length and clarity.

What's the appeal of hiring children to work? Are there not enough workers?

Adults are more expensive labour. Children can be confined [against their will] to work [longer hours], which happens in Bangladesh, Africa, Latin America, Nepal. Children are preferred because of that.

It's hard for consumers to know whether products were made by children, but you helped come up with a solution for carpets. In the 1990s, you supported Rugmark,

a special tag for carpets made free of child labour. How did it work?

I talked to Congressmen and Senators and trade unions and said: "If you keep using those carpets in your drawing rooms with pride that these beautiful hand-knotted carpets were made in Pakistan, Nepal or India," you are responsible for the perpetuation of slavery.

I told them: "I am not asking you to boycott all those carpets. I'm asking you to buy carpets which are guaranteed to be free of child labour."

Today, we have seen the decline of child labour in the three countries where we have been working. In 15 years, it has gone down from one million to hardly 200,000.

Through your charity, Save the Childhood Movement, you staged rescue missions to free over 83,000 children and adults working in slavery. Can you tell me about one kid who made an impression?

There was a child I freed from the carpet industry in India. His name was Kalu. He was enslaved for about six years and he was freed by me in a very risky operation. At that time, he was about 11 or 12.

He was a bright child. He lived in one of our three rehabilitation centres, where he went to school. He topped his class and helped other children, so we promoted him.

In the last days of Clinton's presidency, I invited Kalu to join me at an event with President Clinton [in Washington, D.C.]. By that time, Kalu was 13 or 14. Kalu said to Mr Clinton: "You are the most powerful person on Earth." The President smiled. "I am fortunate enough to be freed, but you as the president can do much more. What are you doing for children like me?"

Did President Clinton do anything?

Within a week, the US increased its support to the ILO for the eradication of child labour from $ 6 million to $ 30 million. That was pure leadership on Kalu's part. If given an opportunity, these children can speak truth to power.

You believe child labour can lead to extremism.

If you stop children from entering good, quality-free education, you are creating more tension and violence in the world. The illiteracy and exploitation of children, the growing inequality of children, is the most serious threat.

These children can be brainwashed for extremism or terrorism. They're vulnerable. If we were investing enough in education in Afghanistan, India, Pakistan, where we see these problems, we might not be facing threats today.

Is all child labour bad? In some cases, children bring much-needed income to their families.

That is the most commonly asked question. All child labour is bad.

An actor named Boman Irani is playing you in an upcoming Bollywood film called *Jhalki*, which is about a girl trying to free her brother who has been trafficked for child labour.

This man playing my role has never met me, but he has fallen in love with me! The other day, he said [he was] watching my YouTube speeches and [videos about my] life. He knows more about me than many of my peers.

What message do you have for Americans?

I would like to appeal to the President and the administration: "No problem in the world can be solved in isolation".

America is not on a different planet. If we want to create a secure world, we have to send a message across the world that all children are our children.

The children who are victims of slavery or trafficking, the vulnerable seeking refuge in other countries, they are our children — be it Syrian, Afghan, Yemeni. This should be the strong message from a country which has been championing human rights and democracy.

❑

12

End Silence around Child Labour

- Child workers have gone down from 26 crores to 17 crores in the last 15 years: UN.
- The number of children out of school has gone down from 13 crores to six crores.
- End your silence around child labour; consider all children as your own.

Kailash Satyarthi has been a campaigner for child rights nationally and internationally for three decades. His 'Bachpan Bachao Andolan' has laid particular focus on freeing children who are forced into exploitative labour or servitude. His work has been amply recognised and honoured, particularly internationally. In 2014, Satyarthi shared the Nobel Peace Prize with Malala Yousafzai of Pakistan.

While top awards have crowned his efforts, they have not capped them. His campaign against child labour continues. He is currently working to launch a campaign called 'Hundred Million for Hundred Million', which is aimed at the youth across the world.

In a free-wheeling chat with NDTV, Satyarthi talks about his life and work. His message to the ordinary folk is: 'Just break the silence over child labour.'

In addition to your long-term campaign against child servitude, what's keeping you occupied nowadays?

Currently, I am preoccupied with getting amendments introduced to the Child Labour (Prohibition and Regulation) Amendment Bill that Rajya Sabha passed on July 19.

The Bill has two main faults — firstly, it reduces the number of industries considered hazardous for children from 83 to just three; and, secondly, it allows children below 14 to engage in home-based work. So, the families will be allowed to use children in such work.

These two faults should be removed before the Bill is considered for passage by the Lok Sabha.

Tell us about 'Hundred Million for Hundred Million' campaign.

I am working on launching the campaign called 'Hundred Million for Hundred Million'. There are about 100 million children, youth and girls in the world who are victims of violence, malnutrition, sexual exploitation or are not receiving any education. We want another 100 million young people who have food, security, education and good prospects in life to become the voice of their 100 million unfortunate counterparts.

We plan to reach out to the youth through social media, academia and groups and associations of the young. The plan is to launch the campaign by the end of the year.

To which event or moment in your life do you trace the start of your work against child labour?

I was five-and-a-half years old. It was my first day at school. Outside the school, I saw a boy of my age stitching shoes. The questions that I then asked to my teachers and family members did not provide any satisfactory answers.

As a child, I would raise money to help poor children pay their schools fees and buy books.

After completing my engineering, I worked only for a year-and-a-half before deciding to make stopping child labour my life's aim. My wife has helped me throughout in that work.

How has the Nobel Prize smoothened your way?

Nobel Prize has made me much better known nationally and internationally. I no longer have to wait for months to get an appointment with an Indian or foreign leader. I have now been meeting Presidents, Prime Ministers and other top decision-makers to help me in my work in their countries.

The issue I deal with is one of the lowest priorities in most societies. I have been successful in taking it to the topmost echelons of decision-makers. That's a great moral responsibility that I cannot avoid.

The most significant change that Nobel Prize has brought is the inclusion of child labour, child slavery and violence against children in the sustainable development goals.

What can an ordinary person do to stop child labour and how?

First thing for ordinary people to do is to end their silence. Consider all children as your own children. Talk to your local MP or MLA. Use social media. Start protesting at places where children have been employed.

Awareness will bring change across the world as is evident in the change we have already seen. The United Nations statistics show that the number of child workers has gone down from 26 crores to 17 crores in the last 15 years. The number of children out of school has fallen from 13 crores to six crores.

Europe is facing a migrant crisis that has put in relief the plight of children. How does your work touch that issue?

My wife and I have recently been to a migrant camp in Germany where I learnt a lot from the children and got an insight into their plight. I saw dreams in their lives even though their families lost everything they had. I also spent a day in a migrant camp in Turkey.

The flood of migration means children are being deprived of food, security and education. Many of them are being enslaved, some are being pushed into crime, some just disappear. In conflict-ridden Syria alone, 20 children disappeared.

I raised the issue with many Heads of State and ministers and urged them to open their borders to the children in distress. I also raised the issue at the UN Humanitarian Summit in Turkey. A campaign called 'Education Cannot Wait: A Fund for Education in Emergencies' was also started during that summit to help distressed children get education.